Living in the Shadow of Death: From a Child of War to a Soldier of Christ

Samuel Patrick Okurut and Charity Cherise Okurut

ISBN-13: 978-1976108945
ISBN-10: 1976108942

LIVING IN THE SHADOW OF DEATH:
FROM A CHILD OF WAR TO A SOLDIER OF CHRIST

Dedication iii

Acknowledgements vii

Introduction ix

Forward *by Charity Cherise Okurut* xi

PART ONE xv

Ingoratok: People from Ngora 1

Hide and Seek 7

Escape to Soroti 13

Living in the Battlefield 17

Respite in Katakwi 21

Life in a War Camp 25

A Shallow Grave 31

Lu Ojok Tau: My Childhood Heroes 37

Witless Pupil 41

Forced to "Eat Jesus" 43

Digging for shoes 45

Another War - But Not Against Flesh 53

Steven and a Dream Come True 57

Great Ambitions in the Slums of Kampala 67

Safe House 71

Lessons for Dying 81

Scars 87

PART TWO 93

Interviewed by my Future Wife 95

Freedom in Forgiveness 101

Lessons for Living 105

A Father to the Fatherless 109

Habitat 115

A Gentle Whisper 121

Bride Price 129

Epilogue 141

Afterword *by Charity Cherise Okurut* 145

The Father's Heart Foundation 147

A Ministry Overview *147*

About El Salvador *147*

History and Culture *147*

Our Mission *150*

Sustainability *152*

Board of Directors and Ministry Partners *153*

How to Partner With Us *154*

Missionary Teams *154*

Sustainability Discipleship Farm *155*

Family, Childcare and Education *155*

Serve as a Board Member and Network on our Behalf *155*

Pray *155*

Invest in Sustainability *156*

Charity's Testimony 157

What Must I do to be Saved? 162

DEDICATION

We live in such a way that no one will stumble because of us, and no one will find fault with our ministry. In everything we do, we show that we are true ministers of God. We patiently endure troubles and hardships and calamities of every kind. We have been beaten, been put in prison, faced angry mobs, worked to exhaustion, endured sleepless nights, and gone without food. We prove ourselves by our purity, our understanding, our patience, our kindness, by the Holy Spirit within us, and by our sincere love. We faithfully preach the truth. God's power is working in us. We use the weapons of righteousness in the right hand for attack and the left hand for defense. We serve God whether people honor us or despise us, whether they slander us or praise us. We are honest, but they call us impostors. We are ignored, even though we are well known. We live close to death, but we are still alive. We have been beaten, but we have not been killed. Our hearts ache, but we always have joy. We are poor, but we give spiritual riches to others. We own nothing, and yet we have everything.

2 Corinthians 6:3-10

Rejoice in our confident hope. Be patient in trouble, and keep on praying.

Romans 12:12

I WOULD LIKE TO DEDICATE this book to all who have found themselves bruised, bleeding, cheated, deprived, condemned, broken, and cast down in this journey called *life*. Regardless of where you are in this journey, please know that there is a Creator who cares deeply about His creation - whether or not you know Him or believe in Him yet.

My prayer is that through this book, you will witness God's hand of protection, providence and deliverance. And as a result, I sincerely hope that you may be drawn to seek to know the Lord Jesus Christ as your personal Lord and Saviour.

Is there anything good that could come out of following Jesus? Read and see for yourself! This book is a testament of God's unfailing love and grace. He alone is worthy of our praise and honour.

This book is also dedicated to our children: Benjamin, Eleanora, Eseuna and Charity. May you each come to know and love the Lord your God with your whole life. May you each have your own personal testimony of salvation and of fruit that lasts - a testimony of the goodness and the character of God, that you can share with everyone you meet.

ACKNOWLEDGMENTS

FIRST AND FOREMOST, I WOULD like to thank God, for He is the Author of life and He is present and involved in all of our stories.

I would like to thank my amazing wife, Charity, for the hundreds of hours she has spent putting all the different pieces of my story together and turning them into the book that you are now reading.

Charity, you are a gifted teacher, writer and story teller. Amidst all that life has thrown at us, you have been there, juggling the demands and pressures of life as a missionary wife, a mother, home school teacher, home maker, and author. I wouldn't have been able to sit down and write even one sentence of my story, because my past is not a place I go to easily or naturally, but rather a place I tend to avoid. Thank you for getting into my shoes (emotionally) and capturing the details of this story, I am blessed and glad that now instead of agonizing through the details of this story I can still share it without opening my mouth.

And, I am so thankful for Misty Thomas, and also Adrienne Mugwanya for giving of their time and talents to edit and proofread this book, and to be an encouragement to Charity in the final stages of making this book a reality. We really appreciate you both.

I would also like to thank everyone mentioned in this book, who has played a part in my life in one way or another, I am who I am today because of the teachings, encouragement, the friendships, love, counsel and all the conversations that you were part of. Thank you.

I would especially like to thank my parents, Mr. Micheal Egiru and Asire Cicilia, and Toto Jane. Also, thank you to all of my Ugandan and Canadian family.

Thank you to the Red Cross, its supporters and volunteers, and to all those who bring relief to internally displaced people and refugees. I would also like to thank Uncle Tom Herskowitz, Uncle Jones Bakimi, Uncle Jay Dangers, and everyone that I met at New Hope Uganda, Ronald Ongopa, Collin Semakula, Scott Metzel, and everyone at Habitat for Humanity Uganda, Chris Sperling and family, Pastor Josh Carlson and the leadership of Calvary Chapel Kampala.

Finally, we thank God for each congregation and individual who has supported us through prayer, and through finances as we serve God on the mission field - we really appreciate each one of you!

INTRODUCTION

THE BOOK THAT YOU ARE holding will bring you back with me to my childhood: to the joys of being a young boy on my Papa's farm in Uganda, to the traumas of war and the struggles of life that have brought me to where I am today.

The purpose of writing this book is to be a testimony, bringing glory to God. Through every adversity, through all of the trials and testing of my faith, God was there and He was and is on His throne. He is there in your life too.

In the middle of a torture chamber back in 2002, I promised God that if He would free me, I would tell everyone that I would meet about what He did for me. I hope that now, with this book, I can fulfil that promise to God in an even greater way, by declaring through print God's power and His mighty acts, even to those to come.

My life story includes descriptions of war and torture, so is not suitable for young children. Sensitive readers may wish to skim over pages 71-86.

FORWARD

by Charity Cherise Okurut

I WAS THERE IN UGANDA, the evening when Samuel first shared how he had been harbouring unforgivingness for those who had orchestrated three and a half months of torture for him and his cousins. I could see the pain in his face and hear the bitterness of his soul as he wept and confessed the hurt and hatred that he had carried. I could also see some of the scars from his torture, the most obvious one being a large keloid on his neck, about the size of his thumb, which he explained was from a whip.

While I was impacted by his story, the depth of his grief and the struggle to forgive, I could not know the profundity of the healing that began that day, nor how my own story would become so intertwined with his. That was 13 years ago, and our stories have now become one.

I learnt a new respect and gratefulness for the man of integrity that my husband is, in light of all that he has experienced. And, I am thankful that he doesn't hold tightly to his tribal culture, but seeks to live out a biblical culture in every area of life.

This is Samuel's story. I am his helper, and in this case, his writer, but this is his story, in his words. I have heard him tell it so many times, learning new details and hearing his heart and emotions behind the words, and then sitting down to research and interview him to learn more. I have walked in his village and seen the mud hut that he helped to build as a toddler. I even crawled through and hid with a camera to photograph the tall grass in which he would "play" hide-and-seek as a child, when the enemy attacked. I have touched his scars. And in writing, I have vicariously lived this story, writing each page while imagining myself to be Samuel and reliving his past as if it were my own.

The first draft was printed in time for our eighth wedding anniversary. Five months passed, and Samuel had not been able to read through it. While God had already done so much healing, it had just been too painful to relive through print, and we were just coming out of a time of being completely burnt out on the mission field. Several close family members had also died, including Samuel's maternal grandmother, some cousins and his only surviving brother – who left behind five children. He couldn't bring himself to edit the book.

The first weekend in November 2016, we spent time together at a missionary conference in El Salvador, while our four children stayed with my mom and family in Canada. The theme of the conference was "Resilience in Ministry".

It had been a few years since our faith and calling had been tested by things like the near drowning of our daughter and having our lives threatened by criminals masquerading as gang members in El Salvador. By the time of the conference, we were near the end of what had turned out to be a difficult and trying, extended furlough. What we thought was going to be a time of rest and refreshment felt more like a "Job experience" filled with loss, want, feeling rejected and depressed, walking though PTSD with our daughter, sickness, my near-death from Malaria, spiritual battles and even boils (with a few glimpses of hope and times of blessing). We were longing to return to the vision that God had given to us, but we were not quite ready yet.

Samuel woke me up at 5:30 am on Sunday, November 6, 2016 to go for a two-hour prayer walk on the beach before breakfast.

As we walked hand in hand on the same Salvadoran shore where we had become engaged 9 years earlier, my mind wandered back to his proposal. While I can't remember the exact words that he spoke, I was impressed that his proposal was saturated with words of serving and worshiping and bringing glory to God. After I said yes, we stood in the crashing waves, and he prayed and committed our lives and relationship to God.

Now 9 years later, we walked the same beach and cried out to God together. We sang and worshipped to lyrics like, "My hope is built on nothing less than Your great love, Your righteousness…I will not walk another way, I trust Your Heart, I trust Your Name…I'm holding on to You." We recommitted our life, marriage, family and ministry to God, determined to do what He has called us to, no matter what. Samuel remarked that he doesn't want to reach Heaven and stand before our Lord, only to be asked why we failed in our calling and blame it on someone not providing or our not having enough resources. As you will see in his story,

Samuel was taught from a young age to work with what he has been given, and *dig* for what he needs. We were and are determined to work for the resources needed to build a sustainable ministry for orphans in El Salvador, Uganda, and anywhere else that the Lord calls us.

Later that day, at the missionary conference, we were meeting with a Christian counsellor. At the end of our time, he asked Samuel if he had ever thought of writing a book! I responded that the first draft was in our hotel room. At dinner, the counsellor introduced us to a book editor who was interested in editing our book. When I flew home to Canada a day later, Samuel stayed behind to meet with our Board of Directors and take care of other ministry business. He also promised to read through the book. Three weeks later he gave it back to me, filled with notes for editing, to get ready to send to the book editor. As we prepare to publish this book, I couldn't be more thankful that God put us together and made us not only partners, but made us one.

Thank you, Samuel, for trusting me not only to write your story, but to become part of it. I love you and thank God for making you my husband, the father of our children, and the leader of our vision.

PART ONE

Now all glory to God, who is able to keep you from falling away and will bring you with great joy into his glorious presence without a single fault. All glory to him who alone is God, our Savior through Jesus Christ our Lord. All glory, majesty, power, and authority are his before all time, and in the present, and beyond all time! Amen.

Jude 24, 25

1
INGORATOK: PEOPLE FROM NGORA

From one man he created all the nations throughout the whole earth.
He decided beforehand when they should rise and fall,
and he determined their boundaries.

Acts 17:26

MY FAMILY COMES FROM WHAT is now the District of Ngora, in Uganda, East Africa. And before that, as history tells it, my people were traveling for generations. My ancestors originally came from the Mediterranean, which perhaps is why even today our language has some similarities with the romance languages of the Mediterranean. Words such as *emesa* which means "table" in my mother tongue of Ateso, is very similar to the Spanish translation *mesa,* to name but one of many examples. From the Mediterranean, we travelled down through Egypt, Ethiopia - settling in Omo valley, Sudan and then down through Uganda and Kenya. We arrived in Uganda around 1600 AD.

As we travelled, we left settlers along the way, including the present-day Kalenjin, Maasai and Jie peoples of Kenya, the Kuuku of South Sudan, the Karamojong, Kumam and the Iteso in present day Uganda.

The last people to settle, before the Iteso moved on to where we still are today in Eastern Uganda, were the Karamajong. The name *Karamajong* is derived from the phrase *Ekar ngimojong*, meaning, "the old men can walk no further." And my people are called *Iteso*, which means "corps" or "dead people," since the Karamajong thought that to continue on and not settle meant certain death.

My family comes from those who settled in Ngora, which at the time was in the District of Kumi. My Papa moved from Ngora to Amuria as a young boy, where he later purchased around 30 acres of farmland to raise crops and cattle. I was born in the village of Acowa, Amuria, along with all of my siblings and immediate cousins, who are culturally also referred to as "brothers" and "sisters."

The third born of twelve children, I am the firstborn son, after two girls, Apolot Joyce and Asamo Florence. I was born on May 18, 1980, the same year that Obote came back to power from his exile in Tanzania. Although it is said that he committed atrocities during his rule, my family and I enjoyed six years of peace under Obote before the government was overthrown in 1986, and my region was declared a war zone.

My Papa was a great businessman and my very first memories are of the comforts of home and of having all that we needed, although we knew nothing of running water or electricity to this day.

My childhood memories of my Papa are that he owned hundreds of big horn cows, which he bought and sold. It wasn't until I was in my mid-thirties that I finally asked Papa how many cows he had, and found out he only had 18!

Cows have been associated with wealth and prestige in the Teso culture for as far back as history knows, and even in Bible times, cows were attributed to wealth. The national average number of cows per household in Uganda is only 1.37 cows, so 18 is a lot, but not as many as were somehow impressed on my memory. I think that my memory shows how much I was impacted by Papa's cows. I was so small compared to the cows and I felt a huge responsibility in caring for them.

Papa was a respected businessman and he provided for his family through trading cows and raising other farm animals like sheep, goats, turkeys, and chickens. He also grew various crops, purely for consumption at home. Papa would buy cows when the market prices were low, and then re-sell them to make a profit.

My mother, who I refer to as *Toto* in Ateso, used to have so many *gomasi*, or traditional dresses. She had one for every occasion! I remember her wearing one just for cooking, while others were for going to the market or for family gatherings. Papa also bought all of his children the best clothes available.

My Toto, wearing the Ugandan traditional dress, holding my youngest daughter

My very first memories are from when I was only three years old and wanting to help my Papa with the animals. I never even thought to be afraid of the cows or think that they might trample me. Not considering myself a baby, I thought I was one of the men and wanted to do what I saw them doing.

My favourite person in the world was Sudoki. Sudoki worked for my Papa, and I would follow him around. My little four-year-old fingerprints are still in the big round mud hut that I *helped* him build in the family compound.

We worked together collecting the rich red earth that eastern Africa is known for, and was part of the normalcy of my life. Sudoki showed me how to add the exact amount of straw and water to form the perfect mud for construction. I can still remember the cool, wet feeling of squishing mud between my toes as we became human clay mixers.

I even helped make the wood frame for our round house. The most fun was throwing the mud into its place and then smoothing it out until it was just right. More than thirty years later, that hut is still standing.

Aside from construction, I always had a love for Papa's animals. One day, when my Papa and his men had just returned from the market with a small herd of cows, I ran with excitement to meet them. I thought that they needed my help in rounding up the cows to be tied, so I threw myself at the hooves of one cow and wrapped my little arms around her legs to help. My Toto almost had a heart attack!

I know there were many times when I frightened my Toto because I wanted to work with the men. It was only by the grace of God that those animals never injured me!

By the time I was five years old I was given the responsibility of caring for all of Papa's cows on my own. I would open the corral to let the animals out and bring them to graze by the swamp. When it was time to go home, I would call the lead (Ingoratok) by name and he would come running, bringing the herd with him. I had trained them to come by rewarding them with salt bricks to lick. My Papa was astounded at the way the animals were so obedient and comfortable with me. They were more like my pets than livestock.

When my animals rested in the shade at midday I would lay my head down to rest on one of them, much to the surprise of anyone who passed by.

A young boy with his cows, on my Papa's land

I asked Papa about taking care of his cows instead of going to school. I preferred to be with the animals, but I was surprised to learn that I actually had no choice in the matter and was forced to go to school. I would cry as I got ready for school, and my sister Joyce would carry me on her back all the way since I refused to walk 4 km to school! It took some time before I would learn to like going to school, as all I could think about was being with my small herd of cattle.

We had one bull in my herd that was unusually large, and Papa's business colleagues would tell people about him. People would come from all over to see my bull. One day he wandered over to the community well and the women there dropped their clay water pots in fear, assuming that he must be dangerous, because he was not like any other bull they had seen. They were shocked and scared for my life as I calmly and boldly approached what they assumed was a dangerous animal and lead him away.

I named my lead bull Ingoratok, which means *people from Ngora.* To me, the animals were my best friends. I couldn't imagine growing up and doing anything other than care for them.

2
HIDE AND SEEK

The wicked frustrate the plans of the oppressed,
but the Lord will protect his people.

Psalm 14:6

IN 1986, MY REGION WAS declared a war zone, and we began to see the effects of war.

I remember one day bringing the animals to the swamp with my younger brother Peter. I was six years old, and he was just a toddler. We heard fighter jets overhead and could hear the shooting. It sounded like someone continually hitting a tin roof. They flew right over us, shooting randomly in the fields. On our way home, we saw that they had shot up a huge stone that they must have thought was a person. And we heard later that the only deaths from that operation were of two dogs!

Aside from that incident, that first year of war, the fighting was not so close, but we had a greater enemy to worry about - the Karamajong.

The Karamajong are agro-pastoral herders, living mainly in the northeast of Uganda. They are a nomadic people and the majority of them do not believe in anything to do with what we would call *civilization* – including clothes! They also believe that they have a divine right to all the cattle in the world. Therefore, anyone who is keeping cows is ultimately caring for what belongs to them, and so they have the right to come and claim them back at any time.

I had heard of the Karamajong, but had never thought to fear them until I heard the shouting and gunfire the day that they arrived at Papa's farm.

In one day, Papa lost everything. They came with guns and took every last animal, and even clothes and household items.

Some Iteso who lost all that they had in one day died of shock and others, including my Papa, to this day have never fully recovered from the trauma of losing all of their wealth and livelihood, nor from the traumas of war.

In my culture, it is traditional for a groom and his family to pay a bride price of cows for a bride, so during this time, people began giving their children in marriage. I know of one man whose wife grew up with him as a sister because they were so young when her Papa gave her in marriage. His parents wanted to find a wife for their son while they still had cattle to give as a bride price. Otherwise, if they had lost everything to the Karamajong, they would have nothing for their son to be able to marry with.

Families also began to learn how to run and how to hide - including mine. But with five children at that time, our parents could not hide us all in one place, nor could we all run together. We learnt to obey on command and if we were told to run, whether it was waking us in the middle of the night when we were sound asleep or if it was while we were bathing or eating, we would *RUN*.

We learnt to hide in the tall Jaragua grass *(scientific name: Hyparrhenia rufa)*, without leaving a trail of fallen grass behind us. We would sprint towards the grass and into cover, and then get down on our hands and knees and crawl as fast as we could to a good hiding place.

Nothing could stop us from running and hiding because to stop meant certain death.

The first time we ran, I remember that I began running with my Papa and sisters, but the Karamojong were closing in behind us. Papa ordered my older sister to take me so that he could run faster, knowing that if he was caught, he would be killed, but hoping that if we were caught that, as children, we would be spared. My sister Florence grabbed my hand and we ran. As we left the compound and entered the bush I stepped on a thorn and wanted to stop. I was forced along and into hiding, and quickly learnt that I wasn't to stop for anything.

If I got a thorn in my foot, I would quickly sweep my foot over the ground as hard as I could to break it off into my foot so that there was nothing sticking out and I would continue to run with the thorn inside. Today, my feet look like a leopard's skin with so many scars from running in the bush.

We also learnt that strategic hiding and not just running non-stop was the best way to cope with the situation. For example, one time, when we were running to escape, my Toto quickly ran to hide behind an ant hill. She had Caroline tied on her back and Peter holding her hand. They ran towards an ant hill that was surrounded by tall grass, when they reached the ant hill, they quickly ducked down and crawled to hide around the other side of it, so that when the Karamojong ran by, they would not see them or any trampled grass. There were times when Toto was under so much stress to keep the babies quiet, and especially Peter who didn't understand that they could all be killed if he was crying.

A typical ant hill

While most children play "hide and seek" for fun, my siblings and I did it as a matter of life and death.

We lived like this for about a year.

I remember one day when the Karamajong returned and we were unable to run. They came with guns and looted our home, looking for anything to take and demanding animals. They had already taken almost everything that we owned and it angered my Papa that they would now want to come and take more. How could they ask for animals when they had taken all of them?

We were standing in the compound, having been robbed of almost everything that we owned. They had even taken some of our clothes – and they don't even use clothes! I frantically took off my clothes to give them, fearing for my life, even though they hadn't demanded the clothes that we were wearing. Then I heard them demanding what Papa wore, not his clothes, but the very expensive watch on his wrist.

There is a point at which a man can become completely unreasonable, and after suffering so much, would be willing to lose his life over the ownership of a watch. With the Karamajong demanding his watch - the only thing in the world that he owned - he refused to give it to them. If it was not for my Toto, I would have been left fatherless that day. As he refused to take off his watch, the Karamojong knelt down to take aim with a rifle at Papa's head. Toto boldly walked over and removed the watch from his wrist and handed it over to the angry Karamajong.

It was after this attack that Papa decided to move us to a relative's home in the town of Soroti, about 40 kilometres away. We were to walk there on foot.

3
ESCAPE TO SOROTI

*A prudent person foresees danger and takes precautions.
The simpleton goes blindly on and suffers the consequences.*

Proverbs 27:12

BEFORE LEAVING HOME, I RAN to our maize corn field and looked for the best and biggest ear of maize corn that I could find. I knew that I would want to roast it and that it would give me energy for our journey.

It was the only thing that I carried. But on our long walk, that one piece of maize became so heavy. I reached a point when I was so tired, I could no longer carry it and I dropped it on the ground. My Toto picked it up and said that she was sure we would find a place to roast it and that it would give me energy for the rest of our journey.

When we reached the first town, Wera, we stayed in someone's home for the night. They took very good care of us, and they roasted that maize for us and served it along with milk tea and food. I remember that they still had all of their animals. We only spent that one night there to rest our feet. The next day we were able to climb into the back of a big truck to take us the remainder of our journey to Soroti.

Soroti Rock. My region is known for (volcanic plugs) rock formations

We finally reached Soroti where we stayed with Papa's eldest sister, my Aunt Emima Alupo, and her family for almost a year. We mostly stayed with her eldest son Isaac Otai. It was in 1988, after enjoying only a short time of peace in Soroti, that a civil war began in our region.

Again, we survived by running and hiding. When danger approached, we would run and hide, just as we had learnt to do in Amuria. Because my parents had so many young children, our relatives and neighbours were at first afraid to be anywhere near us when it came time to run and hide. But after observing how well we listened and how proficient even the young children had become at hiding, people were amazed and wanted to learn from us, to know how to escape the enemy.

They also began to depend on us to tell them who was shooting, and if and where we indeed needed to run and hide. We had learnt to distinguish between shots fired and know what weapon was being used, who the enemy was, and what distance and direction the shots were coming from.

As we survived again this way, the Karamajong attacks began to extend even to Soroti, and Toto wanted us to go back home.

Back home though, life was still a battle, and we continued to run and hide. Toto would usually run with the younger children and sometimes find an old ant hill to hide them in, while my Papa would take me and hide me somewhere before finding his own hiding spot.

One day, Papa hid me in a hollow tree and told me to stay there until it was safe for him to return for me. It was not the first time that I had been hidden somewhere and told not to move, but this time Papa didn't return as quickly as he usually did. I would often see soldiers or rebels, and sometimes even relatives, run or walk slowly by, but I had been trained not to move.

As I sat in the hollow tree and hours passed by, I was sure that Papa had been killed because he wasn't coming back for me. I felt completely alone in the world. I knew that I couldn't go home on my own in case I met one of our enemies on my way, but I felt like if I remained in that tree that I would stay there forever. Toto didn't know where I was. So, who would come and find me there if Papa had been taken or killed? What should I do? I was terrified and lone in the jungle.

Then I saw an uncle run by, and before he was out of my sight, I impulsively jumped out from my hiding place and ran as fast as I could to catch up with him. He didn't even notice that I was following him until we were miles from home and it was late in the day.

In the meantime, Papa had returned to the tree where he had hidden me, and I was gone. He knew that I would never leave my hiding spot alone, and was sure that I had been taken by one of our enemies. Papa was sure that I was gone forever.

I don't remember my Papa ever telling me in words that he loved me, but I knew his love from his actions, and especially by his reaction to my return, that he loved me so much. He was overjoyed to see me, and while I am sure that I was reminded never to do that again, he did not discipline me for leaving my hiding place. I was so relieved that my Papa was alive it was a joyous moment and that I was back in his arms.

4

LIVING IN THE BATTLEFIELD

He will cover you with his feathers.
He will shelter you with his wings.
His faithful promises are your armor and protection.
Do not be afraid of the terrors of the night,
nor the arrow that flies in the day.

Psalm 91:4,5

IT WAS DURING THESE DAYS, that we learnt great survival skills, and how to hide things. My Toto would dig a hole in the ground and bury a pot full of money, and then cover that spot with manure so that no one would think to check it. In this way, even after the Karamajong had stolen what they could, my parents had been able to hide some valuables, including money saved from Papa's business. He'd never used a bank anyway, but kept his money hidden at home.

We were able to buy a bull and a cow in Soroti before moving back to the village, which would help us to survive later on.

We moved back to our village and had peace for a short time. It was during this time that Caroline was born. I remember my Toto sending Florence and me to get our Auntie to come and help, but by the time we came back with her, Toto had already delivered the baby on her own.

Then our village was declared a war zone and people were being forced into camps called "internally displaced people camps" or "war camps." We now had two more enemies to hide from besides the Karamajong.

Our second enemy became the rebel forces who wanted my Papa to join them in fighting, and our third enemy was the new Ugandan Army, the National Resistance Movement (NRM) who thought my Papa was a rebel. If you were seen walking anywhere, the soldiers would assume that you were part of the rebel group and would shoot you on the spot.

As everyone was being forced into the camps, my parents had heard that other camps had suffered from cholera outbreaks. In some cases, whole war camps had been destroyed. They knew that either way meant death for some or all of their six children, but they preferred to risk death outside of the camps. They decided to move us to the jungle.

We lived in the jungle under a large tree, surrounded by thorn bushes for about six months. The ground was our bed and the leaves were our covering. Even in the rain we had nowhere else to take cover. We would sneak back home to harvest cassava from our garden, and my Toto would cook it with certain reeds that do not create smoke. Our survival depended on our being continuously careful not to let anyone know where we were and to protect ourselves from being seen even from the sky, as there was a threat of being bombed from above.

View of hiding in the grass

I do not know how Papa was able to arrange this during the battle, but he owned a huge net, which had been made for catching large tilapia. He gave it to some fishermen at Kiriki River, about 35 kilometers away, to catch fish. The fishermen would dry the fish and somehow my Papa would receive them and bring them home to our tree in the jungle for us to eat.

The fighting was steadily coming closer. We could hear gunshots continually and see bombs exploding close by. We were living in the middle of the battlefield.

The animals we had purchased in Soroti were kept in the bush, and I was the one to care for them. My Papa did not even want to know where they were, because if he was captured and asked, he wanted to be able to answer truthfully and to save the animals.

The bull was huge and knew me as his master. I took chains from our now unused ploughs and used them to secure the bull to a tree with a padlock in the jungle so that he could not wander away or be taken, if found. I think he somehow knew that he was hiding in the middle of a war zone, and he never made a sound.

After six months of living with six children in the jungle, my parents decided to risk moving to another town called Katakwi. Katakwi was about 50 km away. All of the bridges and roads had been destroyed, and this time there was no truck to bring us.

5
RESPITE IN KATAKWI

Fathers can give their sons an inheritance of houses and wealth, but only the Lord can give an understanding wife.

Proverbs 19:14

PAPA HAD STILL MANAGED, SOMEHOW, to keep a bicycle hidden away, and we piled it with the few belongings we still found at home. The two youngest, Peter and Caroline, would sit on the bike and when they got tired, Toto would carry them while they slept. Then my older sisters and I would get a turn to ride. My parents both walked the entire time, carrying us and pushing the bicycle. The cows followed behind.

A relative, walking a foot path by Papa's home

When we arrived, Katakwi was calm. The war had not yet reached there, nor had the Karamajong. We were able to sell the animals and save some money. We rented a small three-bedroom house and enjoyed peace for about 5 months.

Then one night, the Karamajong invaded the town, and everyone fled for their lives. The entire town was in chaos. We were inside watching people running back and forth in the streets. We didn't run. We watched from the window and actually ended up laughing, maybe as some sort of comic relief, at how people would run in one direction, and then hear gunshots or see the Karamajong and run in the other direction, and end up running in circles.

My papa and Toto decided that it was not safe to run, Then they came up with a brilliant idea. They told us to disorganise our house and make it look like it had already been looted. We turned everything upside down. We took a pile of cotton that was in one corner and strew it across the room and even threw some things outside of the house, to paint the picture that someone had dropped them as they were carrying things away. The small three-room house was designed in such a way that when you opened the front door, the door covered the doorway to the next room and made it seem as if what you saw was all that there was to see. We hid in that room. She also took the doormat, which was dirty and muddy, and hid our money in a plastic bag under it, leaving the front door open. We were all kept safe as the Karamajong came to our house, stepping right on that money, but they never entered.

While we were in Katakwi, in 1988, the Ugandan Government changed the national currency, and one had to travel to Kampala, the capital city, to exchange money so that it did not lose all value. We had heard of people travelling all the way to Kampala and then being followed and killed on their way back. My Papa sent money with a business acquaintance who held apposition in the new government. His name was Atuto.

Atuto came with a military convoy to papa's farm and Papa sat with him to count out bags of money, which he promised to exchange in Kampala. He promised to return the new Ugandan Shillings soon after.

To this day we have never seen Atuto.

Papa's old Ugandan shillings

My Papa kept another bag of money, which he still has. He can be found counting it, sometimes in complete despair. He had been a man of great wealth and still has so much money; yet it is worthless paper, and he has been living in both spiritual and physical poverty since then.

The day after the Karamajong attacked Katakwi Papa and Toto decided to move back home. They resigned themselves to the fact that it was impossible to escape the war, and if they were to be killed, they would rather be killed at home.

We moved back home, and struggled to survive and to hide. Papa was often taken to be beaten, but his life was spared each time. Finally an army Generals commanded the soldiers to leave Papa alone; if he was a rebel, the General concluded, then they wouldn't keep on finding him at home with his family.

Papa and I would go hunting, and one day we were walking close to home, by the main road, when we could have been killed. We quickly ducked down by the side of the road, where it sloped down like a ditch. We counted about 500 soldiers, marching past us. We stayed there until they had all passed, and then waited a little while longer, before slowly making our way to the trading centre close by. There were bodies all over the dirt road, they had killed everyone that they had met in their way. Death was everywhere, and there was no place to hide.

6
LIFE IN A WAR CAMP

*The Lord is a shelter for the oppressed,
a refuge in times of trouble.*

Psalm 9:9

WITH THE WHOLE REGION FIGHTING, my Papa gave up trying to hide and escape the battle, and so he resigned to following the government decree to live in a war camp.

I was around eight years old when I became what felt like a prisoner of war. We were forced to live together with more than one hundred thousand people in a confined space, with no water, no pit latrines or drainage system, and in what used to be a small trading centre of not more than 100 residents. When we first arrived, we had practically nothing, and we were given nothing. It was as if we had been sentenced to death and placed in a mass-grave. Only it was above ground, and though we soon looked like walking skeletons, we were not yet dead.

We had no house, no building materials, no food and nowhere to plant or harvest crops or keep animals. There was no drinking water and no toilets. We were surrounded by death, and almost all hope of survival was stripped away.

An Internally Displaced People Camp, being set up in Soroti Town (2004)

Before nightfall that first day, we collected tall grass and made a makeshift hut using only grass, so that we would have a place to sleep with a bit of privacy.

It was the middle of the rainy season. We were able to build a small hut with grass walls and a grass-thatched roof. We shared the wet dirt floor as our one large bed and would cuddle together to stay warm. Our body temperature dried the floor. We had no beddings or blankets for an entire year in the camp.

The camp where I grew up (still inhabited in 2008, when this photo was taken)

When the rains came, the dirt paths between huts became little streams, and as there were no toilets, these streams were a sewer system. We collected rainwater to drink, but many people died of cholera during that rainy season, and throughout our entire time in the camps.

My grandmother, whom I called Tata also died during this time.

Papa's mother didn't want to live in the camps either. Her mind had been affected by the trauma surrounding her and she lived in the days bygone. When Papa would come and bring her food or check on her she would tell him of a party that she was late for and ask his help in bringing her to see a brother or other relative who was no longer living.

One day, Tata went missing. We searched for her in all of the obvious places, but couldn't find her anywhere. Two weeks went by and we had given up trying to find her.

Then Papa had a dream. In the dream he was asked " You have been looking for your mother, but have you checked in your property under the Etobochon tree?" He said "No". He knew the exact tree in his property. When he woke up in the morning in the war camp he told us all about it and had to sneak out of the war camp alone to check under that tree and he found her body there.

The Etobochon tree that Papa saw in his dream where my Tata was found

My maternal grandmother in 2015

When Papa found her, we went together to see her. As the eldest son, it was tradition that I touch the body – but as I neared her, Papa stopped me. It had been about two weeks since she had fallen there and Papa didn't want me touching her decomposing body, even though her body was already wrapped in cloth.

The camps, we were told, were meant to protect us from the war going on around us, but there were times when the fighting came into the camp too. Sometimes, the government soldiers would trick the rebels by making it appear that they had left their barracks for a time. The soldiers would then come and find the rebels in our camp.

We had market days, when people would come together to barter and trade what they had within the camp. One day a rebel soldier had come to the market to collect what they called market dues *(taxes)*. The government military spotted him and he had run through the maze of huts to try and escape.

At the same time, as I was walking home, between huts that were almost touching each other, I saw a soldier crouched down. The soldier was crouched down by our hut, aiming an AK47 toward a presumably moving target. He had seen the rebel "tax collector" and opened fire. As the soldier opened fire, and bullets flew through the inadequately constructed homes around him. I froze in my tracks.

Government soldiers were also following the rebel from behind, so the soldier who was crouched by our hut, ceased fire when he saw his comrades and then ran off to join them in their pursuit.

When he was gone I quickly ran into our hut. When I got to the doorway I found my sister Joyce crying hysterically, holding her head with blood soaked hands. She had been shot.

After things calmed down, we could see that Joyce was fine. A bullet had grazed past her top lip, burning a thin layer of skin off, but not causing any serious or permanent damage except for the scar.

A little while later, we learnt that when Toto was walking towards the camp after finding a place to relieve her bladder, that same rebel soldier ran past her. As he passed her she heard gunshots and then saw a group of government soldiers running towards her, shooting as they ran.

She was pregnant with my sister Rose at the time and both of their lives were in imminent danger – until the soldier closest to her realised that she was there and yelled to the other soldiers to cease fire! They stopped shooting until they had also run past her.

Death was all around us, from people dying of starvation and diseases like cholera and malaria, to others being caught in crossfire or deliberately shot.

Walking to find firewood, herbs or anything else to eat meant walking through a maze of huts, people and corpses. It also became commonplace to see dogs running with a human hand or other body parts in their mouths.

I remember one day when a huge truck came to collect all of the decomposing bodies around the camp. Bodies were thrown into the back of that truck for burial until it was almost overflowing.

I will never forget the smell of decomposing human flesh; it is a distinct smell that is ingrained on my memory. Many times, I have smelled the remains of a dead animal, but the odour of a decomposing human body is incomparable. Later as an adult, while driving in another part of the country I smelled death, and when I asked about it, I was told there was a shallow, mass grave nearby from a recent gas truck spill, which had burned and killed several people.

Some teachers and parents – anyone with a desire to teach and who had some education decided to bring all of the children together to do lessons under the trees and inside the small church building.

We called it the Learning Centre. We would sit for a lecture and then draw in the dirt floor with our fingers or sticks. The teacher would walk around checking our work with a stick and then we would use our hands to dust away our natural notebooks and begin again.

While at school one day, the fighting came closer. The rebels were on one side of the schoolhouse and the government soldiers were on the other side. We found ourselves in the middle of gunfire. All we could do was lie down on that dirt floor and wait for the shooting to stop.

Amazingly none of us were hurt, although some had slight injuries from pieces of the wall that had fallen on them. When the battle calmed down, we ran "home".

The horrors of death became common place, and even amidst this suffering we learnt to survive. Some families would sneak out of the camp to harvest food from their gardens at home, and in season, others would find fruit.

When Rose was born we became a family of ten and anything that was found to eat had to be shared between us. Even to this day, I do not feel right about buying a snack or eating a meal alone. It is so firmly fixed in my mind that food is for sharing that I can more comfortably go all day without eating than to eat out alone.

I don't know how we survived. Especially Toto. My Toto became so thin and frail and yet somehow, always had breast milk. During the entire war though, my Toto had several miscarriages or stillborn births. I remember one was a baby boy. We buried him near our home.

I can remember climbing a mango tree and bringing home as many mangoes as I could carry, but still we never had enough to eat. So, Papa decided that we needed to venture further outside of the camp.

To go outside of the camp was to enter a battlefield. If either side of the conflict saw us, we would be shot on the spot. Papa knew that to leave the camps meant possible death, but to remain we were certain to starve to death. So, Papa and I became more serious hunters.

7
A SHALLOW GRAVE

*Lazy people don't even cook the game they catch,
but the diligent make use of everything they find.*

Proverbs 12:27

PAPA AND I BEGAN OUR hunt by searching for any scrap metal that we could find – old bicycles, farming equipment, and other previously useful items that had become casualties of war.

Although my Papa had never been trained in the craft of blacksmithing, he somehow just knew how to go about making traps. We would make a small fire and use stones to improvise a blacksmith shop.

Using basic blacksmithing, we were able to make traps. Then Papa and I would say goodbye to our family – not knowing if we would ever return – and we would sneak out of the camp and into the surrounding jungle.

One of the traps that Papa and I made

Papa taught me how to track an animal – searching for droppings, paw or hoof prints. We would identify an animal and study its travel, eating and defecating habits. Some animals always defecated in the same spot; others walked the exact same trail, even months later. We would first study and then find optimal places to lay our traps, remembering where they were so that we could come back and check them. Papa had been hunting since before the war, but had previously used hunting dogs that would not just hunt with him or retrieve animals for him, but that he could send out to hunt on their own and that would return home to let him know that they had a kill.

Tracking an animal on Papa's land (2015)

Without dogs or any weapons, we depended on our calculated laying of traps. Once our traps were set we would sneak back into the camp. We knew what times certain military patrols were and would always be strategic about where we left the camp and where we re-entered. We would split up at times, and I was taught not to return by the same path that I had already travelled by. If we saw rebels or soldiers we would hide.

During my childhood, I learnt to hunt for all sorts of animals and food, including: guinea pigs, Antelopes, deer, rabbits, birds, mushrooms and fruits. And even though most of my childhood was spent in a battlefield and in destitution with a real threat of starvation, I became accustomed to eating meat.

During this time, Papa and I would bring meat home for Toto to cook and would also trade with other families who had been able to sneak out to their gardens and harvest cassava or potatoes chips.

One day, I trapped my first antelope. It was a male Grey Duiker. I was nine years old, but that is when I felt like I officially became a man. After trapping an antelope and providing so much food for my family I was a real man and my Papa would even send me to check traps alone. We each had our own traps and would check them and then meet up at a pre-assigned place.

One day during the rainy season, I was sent to check my traps. It started to rain and I had to run back to cross a creek before it filled with fresh rainwater and became impossible to cross, since I didn't know how to swim.

My feet kept on sticking and sinking as I tried to run, and all of a sudden, I sank through the earth and I found myself in a small pit. As I tried to grasp the edge of the pit and pull myself up, I glanced to the side and saw a human foot! I looked down in fear and saw that I was covered in maggots and was standing in a shallow grave! My feet had sunk through the abdomen of a dead man and I could see his rotting head at the other end of the grave. I was terrified.

I don't know how I pulled myself out of that grave, but somehow, I climbed out and ran again, this time in shock and utter terror. I ran harder than ever before and didn't stop before entering the stream that had now become a rushing river.

Without thinking, I found myself being swept away by the current, and I couldn't swim. As I flailed my arms and tried to find footing, barely keeping my head above the water, there was a fallen tree at the edge of the stream. I caught sight of a tree branch. The branch seemed to reach toward me from above the rushing waters. Somehow, I grabbed onto that branch and was able to pull myself to the other side.

Although I was already feeling exhausted from the run and from fighting the water, I didn't stop. I ran as hard as I could until I reached our old compound. I was so relieved to see my Papa. Papa saw me running and the terror on my face. He frantically asked me why I was running. He drilled me, asking if I had seen the soldiers or the rebels or a wild animal. All I could do was to shake my head, "No".

I was so out of breath and in so much shock, that I couldn't talk. I was still so terrified that I didn't even know what to say.

Finally, I was able to catch my breath. Papa could also see that, even though I had been through the creek, I had the evidence on my skin of having been in a grave. He was able to figure out what had happened and quickly helped me to wash off. Once I was clean, we went to sneak back into the camp.

8
LU OJOK TAU: MY CHILDHOOD HEROES

So you handed them over to their enemies, who made them suffer. But in their time of trouble they cried to you, and you heard them from heaven. In your great mercy, you sent them liberators who rescued them from their enemies.

Nehemiah 9:27

WHEN WE FIRST MOVED INTO the war camp, we went with the clothes on our bodies and a few basic cooking utensils.

I remember that we had one saucepan. We had no bedding, no toiletries and no change of clothes. We lived in that camp for five years, and some families were there for much longer. For almost that entire time, I had no clothes to speak of and all I wore was underwear. When that underwear was left as just threads my papa cut his trousers, and my Toto sewed those trousers together and made shorts for me. It felt good to be covered.

For those five years I never had more than one meal each day, and sometimes we went for days without eating.

Every once in a while, my childhood heroes showed up. We called them, "Lu Ojok Tau," which means, "The good-hearted ones." They came in big trucks that had huge red crosses on them.

They had come once just to register everyone in the camp, and we had heard that they might bring relief.

The first time that the Red Cross showed up with relief, they parked their huge trucks on the soccer field by the military barracks. We could see that they had indeed brought relief. There were huge bags of beans, maize flour and containers of cooking oil. They brought cooking utensils and even blankets.

In an instant, the camp was in utter chaos. Everyone fought to be closest to the truck. We all feared that if we were not heard or seen - that if we could not literally touch the truck - then we wouldn't receive any relief. Fighting to be first seemed a matter of life and death.

It took time for Red Cross personnel to persuade everyone to calm down and to form a line. They already had a list of each person who was registered as living in the camp.

When people finally calmed down, we were able to stand in a line and wait to be served. I waited in that line too. When it was my turn, I was handed a new, warm blanket. I hadn't received anything new in about 4 years. Holding that warm blanket felt so good. Holding that warm blanket gave me hope. I knew, from the moment I received relief from the Red Cross, that not only were they my heroes, but that someday I would be out of that camp. And I wanted to work with the Red Cross and bring relief to others who were desperately waiting for help.

The Red Cross came a number of times throughout those five years. Each time we received food for our starving bellies and a new blanket.

Sometimes though, we knew that they were on their way, but we were told that the Rebels had stopped them from coming by blowing out a bridge or doing something to prevent their trucks and their relief from reaching us. It didn't make sense to us why the Rebels, who all had family members in the camp and who would most likely share food with those who received relief, would prevent help from coming. To us, it was government propaganda, but to the nation it gave more reason to fight in our region.

Whatever the truth, it meant more months of foraging and trying to survive on what was in the forbidden jungles around us.

There was also a foreign missionary team that made it to our village and to our war camp. These missionaries came to teach us songs about Jesus and how He loves us. They also brought me my first uniform. Each student who attended the Learning Centre received a uniform of khaki shorts or skirt, and a shirt. Finally, I had clothes. And again, I had hope: of one day being out of the camp and going to school, and maybe even learning the foreign language that I heard these people speaking.

9
WITLESS PUPIL

He who gains Wisdom loves his own life;
he who keeps understanding shall prosper and find good.

Proverbs 19:8

IN 1992, a peace agreement was signed which brought so many years of blood shed to an end. With the new declared peace in the region, Life had returned to normal for our relatives who lived in Soroti town and my Papa decided that it was time to send his son to a formal school.

I had never lived away from my family, and after having gone through so much together, it was not an easy thing to say goodbye. But I was excited about school and about living a life of freedom outside of the camp. I was thirteen years old.

When I began school in Father Hilder's Primary School in soroti town I was placed in fifth grade. I was, after all, a teenager and tall for my age. But other than the simple learning centre in the war camp, and a few months of my sister carrying me to school before the war, I had never been to school.

I could not read or write, and I had never even held a pencil. I had grown up speaking my mother tongue of Ateso, and here at school, everything was taught in English. I had heard very little English before and could not speak it. It seemed like I had left the war camp for a completely different world, one not without battles.

My teachers thought that I was stupid. They hit me over the head with a stick so hard that I would wet my shorts for not knowing the answer to a question, and they laughed at my mistakes in front of other students. I was ridiculed and abused. But I was at school and determined to learn.

Although I had no comprehension of what was written on the blackboard, I would take out my notebook and copy everything down. It took time, but eventually I taught myself how to read the symbols that I was drawing in my book. Eventually I taught myself to read and write, as well as how to speak English. Now, as we are homeschooling our own children and teaching them phonics, I honestly have no idea how I ever learnt to read without the understanding of phonics.

During my first year at school, I would watch other students play during break. They would run and laugh and jump ropes and kick balls. I would stand and watch. I felt like I had lost my childhood. I felt like an old man, although I was treated like a toddler by the adults around me. And I was unable to play with the children around me.

I didn't pass fifth grade, but I knew that I could repeat it and continue to study, and that one day I would pass.

10
FORCED TO "EAT JESUS"

"Everyone who acknowledges me publicly here on earth,
I will also acknowledge before my Father in heaven…"

Words of Jesus in Matthew 10:32

DURING MY FIRST YEAR OUT of the camp and at school in Soroti, I was staying with a cousin and his family. My cousin was usually at work, so I spent a lot of time with his wife and children. I became like a servant to them.

I walked a few kilometres to school and back, and then would go out again with a jerry can on my head to fetch water. I hand washed my own clothes, as well as their clothes, and I had to serve clients who came to drink the local brew my cousin's wife made.

I was treated badly at school and after school. That year was extremely difficult. There was only one person who showed any love and kindness to me. His name was Steven Omoding, a high school student.

Steven was a neighbour. Every day, on my way back from the spring carrying five gallons of water on my head, I would stop to rest at Steven's.

I quickly learnt that Steven was a Christian. He owned a Bible and was very knowledgeable about history and the Word of God. Any question that I had, he could show me the answer to it in that Bible. After months of stopping there and hearing God's Word I was convicted of my own sin and asked Stephen what I needed to do to belong to God's Kingdom. I wanted the joy and the love that I saw radiating from his face. I wanted the confidence of speech. I wanted the obvious relationship with the living God that I knew he had. I was convicted of my sin and of my need for a Saviour. When Steven explained how I could be saved I very quickly confessed my sin and put my faith in Jesus.

The urgency for my need for a Saviour felt so overwhelming that I literally thought that I was the last to encounter Jesus, and I felt like Jesus was coming back the following day. I needed to know everything Steven knew about God, and I needed to know it all *now*!

Steven gave me a small New Testament Bible with Psalms and Proverbs even though I couldn't ready, That little bible motivated me to learn to read by the end of that year I could read individual words but didn't fully understand what it was saying. And with great joy and an overwhelming excitement I shared my newfound faith with my cousin's family.

I couldn't understand why they were not as excited as I was about Jesus. And my faith was immediately put to the test.

I was convicted not to be an instrument in causing drunkenness, and I knew that I could no longer serve alcohol. But when I told my cousin's wife, she said that if I could not serve alcohol then I would have to "eat Jesus" because I would not be served food at her house.

I was still forced to cook food, but was not allowed to eat it. So, again I spent some days without any food, and for the first time in my life, I trusted God to provide for me. It's a terrible thing to suffer under the sun without a relationship with God. Suffering with God on your side makes every trial bearable with great hope.

God provided through Steven. Whenever he could, which was usually once a day after Steven comes back from School around 5pm, Steven would share a meal with me. It was enough to sustain me until the following day same time. I lived like this for a good part of that first year at school, until my Papa learnt that his relatives in Soroti were not feeding me. Papa came for me and brought me home at the end of the school year.

11
DIGGING FOR SHOES

The wicked are trapped by their own words,
but the godly escape such trouble.
Wise words bring many benefits,
and hard work brings rewards.
Fools think their own way is right,
but the wise listen to others.

Proverbs 12:13-15

I WAS BOTH RELIEVED AND devastated when Papa came to bring me home. I was relieved to be reminded again of his love for me and relieved to be leaving my cousin's home and the abuse that I had received there. But I was sad to leave my studies and devastated to be leaving Steven and his encouragement behind.

How would I grow in my faith? Who would disciple me? Where could I go with my questions about God and life?

Perhaps if I had remained in Soroti at that time then I actually would have become completely dependent on Steven for my faith. God, in His grace, knew that I needed to be utterly alone in my newfound faith to learn utter dependence on God.

When I returned to Amuria, most families were beginning life outside of the camp and back home. My parents and siblings were already settled back on our land, and Papa was learning a new way of living. With no cattle, he would have to dig by hand to prepare the land to grow what we needed.

Papa taught me a great truth during this time. If I needed something, I should dig for it. Whatever need or want that I had could be found in the ground. Although I had always enjoyed working with animals before the war, they were like my pets and it was fun and my form of child's play. This lesson in work was different. This time I learnt to work as a means of survival. But I didn't want only to survive; I wanted to study and excel in something.

For the next two years, Papa and I worked hard together. We worked that land and the first harvest was given to me to bring to Soroti town to the market to sell. I felt the responsibility of those years' worth of potential income resting heavily on my shoulders. As I climbed into the truck to take the produce and Papa confidently gave instructions on prices, I lifted my head a little higher and felt my shoulders broaden slightly. Having Papa's trust meant the world to me and I would not let him down.

I brought that harvest to the market and returned the money to my Papa's hand. I knew that he was proud of me and I knew the joy of working the land.

I also became somewhat of an entrepreneur and began a small business of my own. I bought hens and sold eggs. Then I re-invested my profit to buy more hens and a rooster. Before long I started selling eggs and roasted chicken.

I would slaughter the chicken myself, roast them, and then serve it to the people drinking Toto's local brew in our own compound.

Papa showed me a piece of property to plan cassava, it took me two years of taking caring of my cassava garden before I could harvest it, I bought my first pair of shoes when I was 16 after harvesting and selling the cassava from my garden.

Papa had managed to register me at a local school and I continued my studies while I was home in the village. We had classes under trees, until the Christian Children's Fund (CCF) built their first seven classrooms.

I also continued to study God's Word. I didn't want to remain the same; I wanted to grow in my love and knowledge of Jesus. I still had so many questions and wanted to know what God had to say about so many things.

I would walk to the jungle. It was safe now. I didn't have to run and hide. I didn't have to worry about running into an enemy soldier or rebel with a gun. I could walk peacefully now. I heard sounds that I barely noticed growing up, sounds of beauty. The birds sang and monkeys chattered as I looked for a good climbing tree.

I would find a good tree, climb up and rest in its arms, pull out my pocket Bible and drink in the Truth. Every question that I came up with was answered in that book. Sometimes I would sit for hours until I came across an answer, sometimes it took days before I could get the answer but it was there.

God spoke to me through His Word and I grew, and I changed.

I was determined to finish school and was so glad that Papa wanted me to continue my education. I was given the privilege of going back to Soroti for high school.

Me, (pictured in blue), with two cousins at Toto Jane's home, (circa 1997)

This time Papa sent me to live with my cousin Jane Alupo. Jane was a widow with three children, and although she always had limited resources, she also worked the land and grew what she needed to eat, and to sell as a source of income. And she always took care of others in her home. Jane became like a second mother to me and I even call her "Toto."

Visiting Toto Jane and her mother, Alupo (my Papa's sister), (circa 2006)

I had survived living in the jungle, on the run, and even in the war camp. Now I would learn a new way of survival. Papa's lessons in work and digging up riches did not fall on deaf ears, and I was ready to get dirty and help Toto Jane with anything she needed.

I have since heard many students, especially in North American colleges, complain about difficult schedules and lack of sleep, but I have yet to meet anyone with a schedule that compares to my cousin-brothers' and mine.

I had two cousins at Toto Jane's, and we worked around the clock to cope with surviving at school and at home.

We would be up at three o'clock in the morning to go to the gardens. After working hard for a few hours, we would come home to bathe put on our uniforms and begin the long walk to school no breakfast. After a long day at school we would return home on foot, we eat and immediately go to the gardens. Then we would come home to bathe, wash clothes, eat and then begin our homework. We would go to sleep sometime around ten. If the moonlight was bright, and especially when we were heaping potatoes (to prepare for planting), we would go to the garden around 3 Am after short sleep, otherwise, we would wake with the dawn to begin our day again.

It was a matter of survival. After about a year, I also needed those gardens to continue my education. Papa did not earn enough with the harvest to keep me in school, as well as support nine other children at home.

Toto Jane gave me a portion of land around her compound to grow my own vegetables, and the produce helped me pay my school fees.

I would go to the local food market and look for rotten tomatoes in the garbage bins. I would pick up the rotten tomatoes and egg plants etc.. from the garbage bins in the market. I would go home and get all of the seeds out and mix the wet seeds with ashes and then dry them in the sun. Once dry, I would plant those seeds in a nursery bed and care for them by watering twice a day. After the seedlings had grown, I would transplant them to my garden and watch them grow, taking time to water and weed my garden and make sure that I had a harvest. That harvest helped keep me in school.

Although I spent so much time in those gardens, it wasn't quite enough. I needed to look for other ways to make money. But not having any other time outside of school I had to find a way of making money during school.

I decided to try my hand at photography. I didn't have a camera, and had never even tried to take a picture before, but when you feel like your life and future depends on something, you find a way to make it happen.

I knew of an older student who owned a camera and negotiated with him to rent it and pay him out of my earnings.

Unlike today, and especially in the Western world, students didn't have cell phones or any device to take pictures, and cameras were forbidden on school property.

It is still common in Uganda, even today, at large sporting events, celebrations and ceremonies, that photographers come and take pictures. They have them developed and return at the end of the event to sell them.

I convinced the school director to allow me to be *the* official school photographer. Because my future depended on it, he conceded, and I was the only student on campus allowed to take pictures. I would attend special events and take pictures, sell them, and then pay for the camera rental and developing costs. Any profit went toward my school fees.

As I studied I also began making new friends. I became quite popular and enjoyed the attention of fellow students. In my pride, I began to rebel. I became the leader of a group of students, and we would challenge school rules and stir up trouble.

We never did anything *against the rules,* but acquired a copy of the school rules and would make our own *clauses* to certain rules, looking for any loopholes or incomplete guidelines.

One day, my class had a student teacher. I decided that it would be funny to change our names. So, when the student teacher introduced herself, she asked each student to introduce themselves by standing up and saying their name. It was my turn, I stood up and introduced myself by stating the name of my classmate beside me, and the rest followed suit. Other students began to snicker and giggle, and soon the classroom erupted in laughter. We were singled out and taken outside.

On our way to the staff room where we would be questioned, my classmates, my followers, betrayed me. I couldn't believe that they would turn me in, and let me take all of the blame and discipline. Schools still administered spankings then, and I received about six lashes, and also had to dig out a tree stump.

That was the end of my rebellion. Somehow, receiving that discipline and knowing that I could not depend on those friends, made me realise my sin and how I had not only rebelled against the school rules, but against God. I repented and resolved to follow God with my whole heart. My friends thought, at first, that I was joking.

God also gave me the opportunity to earn money towards my school fees by being elected as Deputy Speaker at school level, and Secretary: Information and Publicity, Uganda National Student Association (UNSA) at district level. Ugandan education includes a model of the Ugandan political system, and even has paid position.

Pastors Desderious and Eloba

As I developed my leadership skills, I became good friends with some Christian brothers who were starting a small church close to my Toto Jane, in the village of Amen. I was involved there too, and became like family to Pastors Desderious Ourum and Eloba Leonard as they discipled me. They also baptised me when I was 18.

Aside from that one year of rebellion, I grew in my love and knowledge of God and was blessed with a community of believers who surrounded me at school. It was a Christian school, with Bible studies and worship times two times every day. I enjoyed secondary school, especially the practical work experience and the Christian fellowship that I had there.

12
ANOTHER WAR - BUT NOT AGAINST FLESH

For we are not fighting against flesh-and-blood enemies, but against evil rulers and authorities of the unseen world, against mighty powers in this dark world, and against evil spirits in the heavenly places.

Ephesians 6:12

Lord, you are my strength and fortress,
my refuge in the day of trouble!
Nations from around the world
will come to you and say,
"Our ancestors left us a foolish heritage,
for they worshiped worthless idols…"

Jeremiah 16:19

BEFORE I HAD EVER HEARD the name of Jesus, and long before I had given my life to Him, I knew that God existed. I knew that there was a spiritual world, but I didn't know that it too was at war.

From my early childhood and even throughout the war, I was exposed to a spiritual power and had been trained to go to the local witch doctor. I was even sent on behalf of the whole village when my family and neighbours fell sick with measles.

I went to consult about what we were to do to be healed. I myself was not sick, but my siblings and parents were very ill. The witch doctor told us to go down to the swamp and perform a ritual involving a chicken and a sacrifice, to appease the spirits that were believed to be causing the illness. We were to do everything exactly as told, and upon reaching home, not look back until after we had entered our huts. Anyone who looked back would annul the appeasement. I was the one to instruct everyone on what the witch doctor had directed.

So, after I had been born again and baptised, I knew that there was a Holy Spirit, the Spirit of God, who Jesus had promised to send to those who believed. I knew that my body is the temple of the Holy Spirit, and that He who is in me is greater than He who is in the world. I also knew from experience that the powers of Satan are real, but they have been overcome. God's power is ultimate.

I hadn't yet learnt the reality of the battle though, and the importance of standing firm in the armour of God. I thought that I was standing firm in my faith, but after several visits home to the village during school breaks, I allowed myself to put down my weapons and protection, and I gave in to my Toto nagging me to help her build a shrine.

Toto asked me every time she saw me to help her. She was being tormented by evil spirits, and they had demanded a place to stay and be fed. She needed a small hut-like shrine to appease them so they would stop tormenting her.

At first, I stood firm. I knew it was wrong. But after some time, when I had just finished firing my own bricks and building my own hut to stay when I was home, Toto convinced me to use the few leftover bricks to build a shrine for her.

After that I had experiences that made me think twice before visiting the village.

I shared a hut with my brother Peter. One day after dinner, I was in bed and talking while Peter made his bed. As I was talking, I felt a heaviness, like a tangible shadow, come over me. Peter continued talking, but I couldn't answer. I could feel pressure being applied to my neck and felt as if I would be strangled to death. Peter watched me, calling my name and asking if I was ok.

In my mind, I knew that I had to say a name, but there was a cloud preventing me from even thinking the name. I fought in my spirit and wrestled with my mind, demanding that I say the name, "J-J-J-Je-Je". I could make out the beginning sounds, but only in my mind. Finally, I could in my mind, but not yet audibly, say, "Jesus."

Peter ran out of the house because he thought I was dead. He called my parents. They came in, and could see me looking lifeless even thought I had very shallow breath, I could no blink or wiggle a figure my Papa and Toto panicked, I was dying, but they didn't know what to do.

I kept thinking that I wished I could tell them to say, "Jesus." Finally, after thinking the name Jesus, I began the same process of slowly being able to audibly say His name. When I finally said it out loud, the heaviness lifted at once. I continued praying and just saying, "Jesus" for the next hour or three.

Another time I was in bed in my little hut, and I saw these six women coming towards me. But they were not normal women. They looked like cartoon characters, with abnormally voluptuous features. I knew in my spirit that they were evil spirits and with the power of Jesus' name being spoken, again they fled.

There is power in the name of Jesus, and every time I felt an attack of evil spirits, I prayed and commanded that they leave in Jesus' name. But every time I came home to the village, I was attacked again.

Then, one day while Papa and Toto were in the market, I was alone at home with my little sisters. I started singing a worship song and crying, tears were just welling up and streaming down my face. Before I knew it, I started looking for an axe. With the axe in my hand, I walked into the compound and felt an overwhelming passion and anger come over me. It is difficult to explain how I felt, but it must have been a righteous anger from God. Without thinking, rationalising or planning in any way, I walked across the compound to where that shrine was. In a rage, I tore it down, smashing the bricks, leveling it completely down. I then pulled the roof outside of the compound and lit that grass-thatched roof on fire. It lay completely destroyed.

I then wondered what my Toto would say.

But to this day, neither Toto nor anyone else at home has ever questioned or mentioned about that shrine or what happened to it. Since then I never got attached again while I was home. The enemy gave up trying to hurt me.

13
STEVEN AND A DREAM COME TRUE

You have decided the length of our lives.
You know how many months we will live,
and we are not given a minute longer.

Job 14:5

Teach us to realize the brevity of life,
so that we may grow in wisdom.

Psalm 90:12

WHEN I HAD BEEN BACK in the village, before building that shrine, Toto had given birth to a baby boy. With seven sisters and only one brother I was thrilled to have another brother.

He was given the name Steven. I had to return to school in Soroti and was happy to be back at school, while still missing little Steven.

This time in Uganda was before cell phones were popular and, even now in my region, we have little electricity and no landline telephone service. I had little to no communication with my family while I was away at school.

Imagine my surprise when one day a *boda-boda* (bicycle taxi) driver came rushing, out-of-breath, to find me at school and bring me to the Soroti Hospital.

(Me) on a boda-boda in Amen, Soroti

I quickly hopped on the back of his bike and he peddled hard, bringing me as quickly as he could – which felt painfully slow to me – to the hospital, where I found my Toto who had sent the boda-boda to fetch me.

I will never forget the feeling of urgency, dread and relief that I had arrived just in time to donate my blood to my baby brother, Steven. He was 2 years old and so frail and lifeless, waiting for someone's blood to add life back to his ailing body.

I hadn't even known that he was sick with pneumonia, or that Toto had brought him on that long, dusty and bumpy bus drive from our village to the city.

The hospital staff had told her that Steven would need a blood transfusion to save his little life. The hospital had no blood in their blood bank. The Uganda Red Cross operates by issuing certificates to blood donors so that when they need blood, they can redeem their certificate and receive the blood that they need. We had never even heard about donating blood before and now our little Steven needed family blood to stay alive and fight the pneumonia that was attacking his little body.

I watched, so full of hope and expectation, as my blood was first analyzed and then transfused into Steven's limp body. We waited to see the life flow back into his beautiful little face. But it didn't. It was too late. My baby brother died as my blood tried to pulse through his veins.

I couldn't understand why they had to wait for my blood. Couldn't someone there give their blood? Couldn't someone else have saved little Steven's life? If only I had gotten the news sooner. If only my blood had been tested more quickly.

Toto thought she would return home with a healthy little boy, but had to return home to bury her baby.

An ambulance brought Toto home with Steven. I went home the next day, and stayed to do the service for his burial. I was the only believer in my village at that time, and I performed the (funeral) service for little Steven.

My baby brother, Steven's grave

I returned to school two weeks later, full of grief and anger, and a new passion. I resolved that if I couldn't save Steven, I would make sure that no other life would be lost because of an empty blood bank. I became determined to keep the blood bank full.

Steven's death made my dream of working with my childhood hero come true. I established a Red Cross youth club at school. I was so zealous about finding blood donors that our school became the leading donor for the Uganda Red Cross in our district. If the Red Cross needed blood, they would look for me at Soroti Central Secondary School, and we would set up a blood donor clinic. I was always the first to give, not waiting the recommended wait time between donations (to have enough blood on reserve).

Living the dream of working with the Uganda Red Cross Society. (I am the tallest in the photo, back row, 4th from farthest right).

Because of my passion and success at setting up blood donation clinics at school, I was elected to be the Chairman of Soroti Red Cross Branch, Youth Council. I worked with volunteers to educate, train, recruit and collect blood across the entire district of Soroti.

I quickly discovered that the reason people had not been donating their blood was because of superstitions and rumours that donating blood can lead to death. I would demonstrate and prove that we were not trying to take their lives, but use their blood to save other's lives, like my brother Steven's. Because of my love for Steven, and the testimony of losing him because no one had given blood, thousands of people gave blood and ultimately thousands of lives were saved.

Soon after I began to work in the Soroti Red Cross office, the branch field officer went missing. He left a note, saying that he had gone to the village and would return the following day. When he didn't return, people became suspicious, and when I reported it to the police, they took me as the primary suspect, accusing me of taking his life, so that I could take his position. I was allowed to continue my

Red Cross operations, and even sit exams for National Exams, but I was put under "house arrest" at Toto Jane's. I had police and military keeping me under surveillance for five months. They also forced me to walk for miles and to dig up potential burial sites. His body was never found, but after five months, he was found alive, in another area of the district, where he had gone to search for mercury (which he thought would make him rich).

During those five months, under surveillance, and finishing high school, I remained passionate about working with the Red Cross. I was so zealous about collecting blood, that even without Red Cross facilitation, I worked tirelessly with youth volunteers, to mobilise people, and collect blood. During my campaigns, I collected 1,000 units of blood in 30 days. That month set a record at a national level and I received recognition for it, but I had not been receiving any financial help from the Red Cross, in five months.

The blood bank officer at Soroti Hospital, who would call on me whenever the hospital needed blood, knew of the situation and advised me to write a letter to the Regional Director (who should have been facilitating my office with the funding that he received from the head office). The blood bank officer advised me to copy the letter to each of the Regional Director's superiors. Even before posting that letter, I had drawn national attention, and Red Cross wanted me to help with training in a Disaster Relief Conference. I was also reimbursed for those five months.

When it came time for the National Disaster Relief Conference at Soroti Flight School, the Regional Director told me that I was not invited to attend and should remain at the office instead of hosting them since they were meeting in my district. During the conference, people started asking where I was. They all came to find me at the office. The Regional Director's corruption was uncovered.

The Uganda Red Cross gave me a motorcycle, a Honda 125 XL, to use in mobilizing for measles vaccinations, tracing of missing persons and blood donors. I also received Red Cross first aid training, disaster management, and front-line first aid training. I was trained in bringing medical care to the front line in a battlefield, relief to those suffering as internally displaced people (IDP's) and in finding missing people. I organized and led relief distributions to war camps, and used my motorcycle to find missing people and reunite families who had been torn apart for years because of war.

I was also sent as the first man on the scene to investigate areas where we had heard that people were living in war camps, cut off from the rest of the world, because of seasonal floods.

Once after driving my motorcycle for miles, first on main roads and then smaller dirt roads, and then footpaths, and then through jungle towards where we had heard rumours of IDP's, I came across a scene that will forever be etched on my memory.

These people were frantic and desperate for help! They had no drinking water, no food and they needed medical care. I was their first glimmer of hope and they held onto me, not wanting to let me go. There was a man with bullet wounds in his leg, the leg was literally rotten with sickening stentch.

I had to convince them that I had to first leave in order to bring back any support. After taking note of all of their needs and their personal details, like names and ages, I sped back to Soroti and organized the relief to get back to them as quickly as possible. Concern Worldwide delivered water as we arranged for relief.

Speeding around on that motorcycle put my life at risk too. I was determined to bring help as quickly as possible, which meant travelling at high speeds on pot hole littered dirt roads. I felt invincible and knew that God would protect me as I sped to bring relief. I also had full Red Cross protective bike gear which also let people identify the urgency and quickly give way. Once I raced an ambulance driver, who should have seen the Red Cross that I wore and let me pass, but was determined to race, and try to block the path instead, but I eventually left him behind.

The only two accidents that I had while bringing relief were of hitting a goat that jumped in front of me and hitting a chicken. It was more dangerous to swerve and so I hit them straight on. I don't know what became of the goat. I was probably driving at 120 km/hr when I hit it and I kept going. The chicken though, got stuck between the mudguard and my front wheel. By the time I reached my destination, I saw that the chicken was completely gone - just the evidence of blood was all over the bike.

I had my first introduction to the technology of computers and began to learn how to use a computer while working with the Red Cross. I would write up my reports by hand and bring them to a local business, owned by a *Langi* (tribe) couple, downtown Soroti. They offered secretarial services. I would sit behind the typist and watch to see how she opened Microsoft Word and typed up the report for printing. A few times I arrived at the office and the typist wasn't there, but she had told me to open the document for editing. I would quickly open it, but take a painfully long time to type, using one finger and typing one key at a time!

While working with the Uganda Red Cross between 1999 and 2002, I served as the Chairman Branch Youth Council (Soroti Red Cross Branch) national youth representative and also as the Branch field officer. It was such a great learning experience, with formal training as well as life experience. I was responsible for recruiting, training, and coordinating over 500 volunteers. My childhood dream had been to bring relief to internally displaced people, just as I had received relief from the Red Cross. That dream was fulfilled, and I had the great privilege and responsibility of leading the relief distribution operations in all the IDP Camps at the time. The IDPS was not from war but rather from The Karamojong attacks again.

During my time in Uganda Red Cross I also received training on mass communication, team building and management, first aid and disaster preparedness.

I was also introduced to the Spanish language while working with the Red Cross. A colleague was cleaning off his book shelf and gave me a mini English-Spanish Dictionary. I was amazed by the similarities that I saw between Spanish and Ateso, and I began to dream about serving in a Spanish speaking country. I assumed at the time that I would serve with the Red Cross and assumed that one day I would travel to Spain.

My mini Spanish-English dictionary

Near the end of 2001, I received correspondence from the National Head Office. They wanted my accountability for the funds used ib hosting a team from the Swedish Red Cross, that had recently come to partner with us in the twining Pilot program with Soroti Red cross branch and work towards building sustainable offices for Soroti Red Cross Branch. I had helped to host the team, and was usually the one to sign for and account for money. But I had not received any funds for hosting the team. I asked for the Head Office to please check their records again; I had accounted for all monies that I had received. When they checked, they saw that it was my superior who had signed for the money.

When I brought the situation to my superior, he asked me to please account for the money for him, and told me that he didn't have any receipts, so I would need to make them up. He couldn't believe that I wouldn't do that for him, and he became very angry.

A few months later, when we were hosting a conference, he did not want me in any of the meetings. But, when the meetings were finished, some of the Directors were holding a social evening at a nearby hotel. They planned to invite me there, but one man, who overheard their conversation, ran as fast as he could, to find me. He told me that he had overheard a plan to kill me, and not to go to the social event. Sure enough, some men came to invite me, but the youth volunteers told them that I had returned to Amen village.

Fearing for my life, I decided to leave Soroti and travel to Kampala (an 8-hour ride with the national red cross crew). So, I resigned from my position, but not before a new branch field coordinator was recruited to take my place. I am so thankful that I had the opportunity to live out my childhood dream of working with the Red Cross.

14
GREAT AMBITIONS IN THE SLUMS OF KAMPALA

"Don't store up treasures here on earth, where moths eat them and rust destroys them, and where thieves break in and steal…"

Words of Jesus in Matthew 6:19, 20

WHEN I ARRIVED IN KAMPALA, in April 2002, it was with great ambitions. I was committed to continuing my walk with Christ and to serving those in need as I lived out the Gospel. I also knew that I wanted to own my own accounting firm and wanted to make as much money as possible, enabling me to help my family. My goal was to be able to retire by the time I was 35.

I had saved up some money, working for the Red Cross, and was able to continue my education.

Robert and Simon are brothers of my Toto Jane, they are technically cousins of my Papa. My Papa and Jane's mother are sisters. But even though I call their sister, "Mother" in Ateso, in our culture we call each other brothers. I went to live with them in the capital city. They had purchased property in Kisenyi slum in Kampala, Kisenyi is the largest slum of the city. They lived together with their wives and children in a house that had a little shop or convenience store at the front. Although the area where I was living was less than ideal, and I slept in the living room, I was content because I was with family.

Having left my dream job, I now looked for other ways to serve. I quickly became involved in a church in the slums. By the time I had been there for a couple of months, I was an officially working as an associate pastor. I was also able to register a non-profit to help widows and orphans living in the slums, called Slum Women and Children's Association (SWACA). SWACA helped women and children who had been affected by HIV-aids and needed practical help with things like home repairs.

Rebuilding a widow's home, with SWACA (I am inside, wearing grey)

I was enjoying my studies at the Multi-Tech Accountancy Program (MAP), making friends and serving God. I became a Guild Speaker at Multi-Tech Accountancy Program and loved being part of politics too. I was full of hope for my future and full of ambition for school and business.

I could never have guessed that the most difficult testing of my faith was about to come.

15
SAFE HOUSE

"That is why I tell you not to worry about everyday life—whether you have enough food and drink, or enough clothes to wear. Isn't life more than food, and your body more than clothing? Look at the birds. They don't plant or harvest or store food in barns, for your heavenly Father feeds them. And aren't you far more valuable to him than they are? Can all your worries add a single moment to your life?"

Words of Jesus in Matthew 6:25-27

IT WAS JULY 9th 2002, a Tuesday, at two o'clock in the afternoon. I had just returned from my accounting lessons at the Multi-Tech Accountancy Program (MAP) in Kampala and was sitting down to lunch at my cousins' home where I was living. I sent my nephew Owen to fetch his Uncle, my "brother-cousin" Simon. Owen went to his Uncle's bedroom and came running back, passed by me without answering my questions of what was wrong, and ran out of the house.

It was then that I heard men's voices coming from Simon's room. As I neared the room I overheard Simon pleading, "Kill me here, so that my children can see my body" (*knowing* that he would later be killed and have his body dumped, preventing his family from ever knowing what happened to him).

I entered the room and saw a man holding a short firearm pointed at Simon. He led Simon out of the room through another door, leading through Simon's shop and out to the street. Thinking that I was alone in the room, I was shocked to be hit from behind and shoved down, following Simon from behind. As I was pushed from behind, I did not have time to think or to duck through the doorway, which my 6'3" height could not allow me to walk through. I hit my head so hard on the metal doorframe that everything turned red and then blue and then white, and then I peed through my pants.

When I reached the front porch, I saw Simon and my other cousin, Robert, seated and tied, being held at gunpoint. The thing that scared me the most at this point was being put at gunpoint by a drunken man. Then we realised that these men, although in civilian clothes, were military. We later found out that about three circles of military men in uniform surrounded the house.

During this entire time, we were being questioned as to where we were hiding "the guns." We had no idea what guns they were talking about. Personally, I had never held a gun, despite growing up in a war camp.

We were each blindfolded with a black *Kaveera* (plastic shopping bag). Our arms were tied behind our backs in what is called a "three-piece tie" - in such a way that our elbows were touching each other, with the ropes cutting into our flesh the most effected was simon.

I kept peeing and tried to stop, wondering where it was all coming from. It was a sign of the terror and the shock that I was going through.

By 5 O'clock, we were still being beaten and I wished that I had eaten the food that I had left on the table.

I couldn't put together an eloquent prayer, but kept saying, "Jesus," crying out for Him to save me.

Although we are all over six feet tall and my cousins were very well built, we were expected to sit side by side, with a guard on either side of us.

Before I realised that I needed to move over for a guard to sit beside me, and unable to see it coming, as my eyes were blindfolded, I felt the butt of a gun slam into my chest. I felt as though my chest had been broken open as I doubled over in pain, and squeezed further into the car.

I had been in Kampala for only four months and had a limited knowledge of the city, as my daily routine only brought me to school and back home. So, after we had been through a few round-a-bouts, I had no idea which way we were travelling or where we were going.

When we arrived at our destination, a house which I later learnt was the head office of the Internal Security Organisation (ISO), we were met at the gate by men ready to beat us with batons. We were hit down to the ground and then yelled at to get up and walk, only to be beaten down again. I don't know how long it took us to finally reach the doorway, where others were waiting to question and beat us. After being tortured and questioned about the guns that we supposedly possessed, we were led to what we were told was a "safe house."

The safe house was about three feet high, three feet wide and about 8ft long – like a long concrete coffin. My cousins and I were shoved into this "safe house" with two other men. The walls of the safe house were painted red with blood. We were squished together, and couldn't sit or easily move.

Immediately, we struggled to breathe, as oxygen entered only from three small holes in one side of the tiny concrete cubicle. The holes were between the safe and the main house, there was no oxygen or fresh air coming in. We took turns sniffing air from under the heavy metallic door and the five of us took turns to breathe. The heat and the lack of oxygen became unbearable as the pain of our torture and the ropes that still dug into our arms caused excruciating pain and exhaustion.

We remained in this safe house for five days and were called out every day, for what we were told was "tea time." The "tea" that we were served was a time of torture, which lasted until our torturers were too exhausted to torture us anymore.

Simon, the biggest of the three of us and who was physically a threat to his captors because of his well-built body, had been tied the tightest and probably would have lost his arms, except that - praise God! - I had served with the Red Cross and knew how to alleviate the pain and stop the clotting blood through massage. Without water and soap, or any oil, it took time for me to break down the clotting blood and allow blood to flow through his arms and hands and the process was extremely painful. We were also able to untie and then more loosely re-tie ourselves, knowing that our decision to do so could cost our lives, but we did not have any other choice or we could have lost our arms.

At one point, Simon was giving up on life and begged me to take care of his children when I returned home, knowing that he wouldn't make it. I questioned him then, wondering if maybe he really was guilty. I turned to him and said, "Do you have any guns?" Simon reminded me of how I had lived in their home for four months and was not restricted as to where I went in the house. He assured me that if he had any guns (an "armoury", as we were accused of hiding), I would have known about it. With that I reminded Simon that, "if the truth is that there are no guns, then that truth will set us free." I was not prepared to die for being falsely accused.

But I too became discouraged and in my pain and fighting to breathe, I remember turning to my cousin and asking, "Can there really be life here?" Up until this time in my life I had never noticed my need for oxygen and, like most people, I had taken for granted the fact that oxygen is provided at no cost. But in that safe house, I cried tears for oxygen, wanting so badly just to be able to breathe, feeling death and not wanting to die.

Imagine yourself diving into a swimming pool, and when you are at the bottom of the pool, your body prompts you for oxygen but you cannot get your head out of the water. You feel like your body has trapped you, there is a desire, an urge to escape the trap (the body) such that you can get out, and breathe fresh air. That is how we felt in that safe house. The lack of oxygen made us feel drowsy, and we were continually yawning for lack of oxygen.

All of a sudden, during one of our "tea" times in those five days, Simon exclaimed, "I know now who is killing us!" We then saw that the soldiers were talking to one of our neighbours, a man who had a grudge against my cousins over some land that had been sold to them. He'd made claims, after the seller had passed away, that a portion of the land was his, and that he wanted it back. This man worked as an informer and so he falsely accused my cousin through the Internal Security Organisation, which was investigating the possession of illegal arms in the city, providing a way for him to wreak vengeance on my cousins and take their land by reporting that they owned an armoury – and were providing arms to all of the thieves in Kampala. After Simon exclaimed that he knew who was killing us, one of the soldiers came over and slashed Simon's back with a knife.

After five days in the safe house we were blindfolded and tied two-by-two and then beaten again. Being tied together and unable to see where the next blow was coming from made the torture even worse, as the body's natural response would be to protect itself and even with hands tied, to tense muscles in defensive anticipation to prepare for a blow. Unable to see where the next blow was coming from, we could not even tense our muscles and so we had no natural defense left, which made the beating even worse.

Unable to lift my hands to protect my face, I prayed that no whip would hit my eyes. I had a small scar on my neck, which was caught by the rounded tip of the lash. The whip scooped out the flesh on my neck, causing fresh pain on an old wound.

When our torturers were tired, we were pushed into a vehicle. I suspected it was a van because I could hear the sliding door close. We were driven around for about twenty minutes before arriving at another house. New soldiers were waiting for us. Still tied two-by-two and blindfolded, we slowly made our way from the gate to the front door of this house whilst continually being beaten, kicked falling down, and struggling to get up or to crawl. Somehow, we made it to the house, where we were led into another room and again greeted by fresh torturers.

After being tortured again until we could feel their sweat dripping on us and they finally became too tired themselves to torture us any more, we were locked in to our cells. Each cell was a small, eight-by-eight- foot room. Unlike a typical North American prison, these were just rooms in a house, with a regular door, not bars. In this small room, we joined other men, also charged with possessing illegal arms. In total, we were twenty-two men in an eight-by-eight- foot space.

Again, we struggled to breathe, as the little oxygen allowed into this space had to be shared. There was just a small ventilation brick, a small unopened window, which was out of reach and there was a crack under the door, where any air could enter the room. After we had been beaten and tortured over and over again, our open flesh began to cause this tiny room to smell like a butcher's shop.

Still tied two-by-two we were able to turn our bodies and figure out how to first untie and then re-tie our ropes so that they relieved pressure and allowed blood flow

After having been starved for five days, in this new house we were finally given food. Once a day we were served a small serving of *posho* (a typical East African dish of maize flour and water cooked to the consistency of dough or bread) and between five and fifteen beans in about a table spoonful of sauce or water – which was the only water that we received each day.

We continued to be tortured and interrogated every day. Some men were beaten with batons and whips, while others were tortured by other methods, such as crushing their toes between two dumb bells or ripping off fingernails with a pair of pliers. It was a form of torture watching other men receive their torture too!

While we were there, they arrested Simon's brother-in-law, Junior. He had been working as a shopkeeper for the little shop in Simon's home. He was only fourteen years old. As he stood in the cell, and was interrogated, he didn't even know how to answer. He was shy and in shock and completely terrified. When he didn't answer his interrogator, he was hit hard and blood sprayed from his chest. After a day of interrogation, they moved him to another cell.

Very often, men in the cells were called out in the night and then we were brought the local newspaper the next day to read a headline of a body found somewhere in the city. By the clothing on the body we would recognise that it was a fellow prisoner, whose name had been called the night before. Some prisoners confessed to hiding guns that they could not prove existed, just to have a break from torture and drive to a site where they were supposed to have hidden the weapons.

I was tortured until I could feel pain no longer. The body reaches a point while being beaten, especially on open wounds, that pain is no longer felt. I would be told to lie down and then have my backside beaten. The rule was "twelve lashes without touching" or protecting yourself. For every time that your hand reached out to protect your body the number of lashes would double. If my torturer became tired another soldier would replace him, until they were all tired and I would be pulled back to the cell.

One day in the cell felt like a year.

One of the worst forms of torture was that we were not allowed to sleep. Not just that we were squished together, with no space to lie down and sleep. But we were forced to stay awake, with the knowledge that sleeping was an offence punishable by death!

I think that they must have tied something to the door so that they could easily shake it. Sometimes they would knock on the door or rattle the doorknob. They would stomp down the hall and cock their guns, ready to punish those who may have dozed off. We were always alert, never at rest. Lack of sleep and being constantly watched and kept on alert keeps the body in a constant state of anxiety over impending danger. Sleep deprivation affects the mind in a way that physical torture cannot. While the physical torture can somehow be mentally *escaped*, one cannot evade the torture of being denied sleep.

Sitting in that cell, smelling the open wounds and hearing the laboured breathing of those in the room around me, unable to escape the pain or the mental anxiety and struggling to breathe, I cried out to God from the deepest part of my being.

I could hear the birds outside the window and I envied their freedom. I could recall the scriptures and I was reminded of the verse that says to look at the birds of the air and to see how our Heavenly Papa cares for them, and to know that if He cares for them, how much more for us, whom He values more than the birds. I could not feel that value or His care, I felt abandoned by my Papa God, and I began to question Him and question why He was allowing me to go through this.

Why would He allow the birds outside this prison to swim in an ocean of oxygen and starve me of a simple breath! I cried out to God, that I would love to go through this torture if it was for the sake of His name, if it was persecution for being a Christian. But I could not understand why, if He loved me, He would allow me to be tortured for something that I didn't do.

16

LESSONS FOR DYING

They long for death, and it won't come.
They search for death more eagerly than for hidden treasure.
They're filled with joy when they finally die,
and rejoice when they find the grave.

Job 3:21-22

AS I PRAYED AND CRIED out to God, my cousins chided me for crying tears. "Your body needs those tears, you have no water to drink and will lose more strength." I replied that those tears brought me strength.

I feared death until it became the deepest desire of my heart. Fearing death is about fearing what is being left behind; not wanting to leave this world or worrying about family left behind. I died to those fears. I begged God to reveal to me why I was experiencing this torture, and He remained silent. Finally, I made a feeble promise to God, not boldly and with faith, but as a last hope and out of great weakness. **I promised that if He would save me out of this cell - out of this torture - that I would tell everyone I meet about His deliverance and about His faithfulness.**

I felt pain until I could feel no more. Then I reached a point where all that I wanted to know was how it would feel to die, and then to be relieved of this suffering and be welcomed into His presence. I was ready to die. I gave up on this life, on all of my hopes and dreams and ambitions. I confessed every sin that I could think of. I surrendered completely to God and wanted to be with Him. There was nothing left, but a man *destined* to die.

It took so much energy just to breathe and I wished that I could will myself to stop. If I could even take a five-minute break from breathing! But God held my life and my every breath in His hands. Although it took so much energy to breathe, I was not willing myself to breath nor could I will myself to stop. God sustained my breathing and commanded my body to keep living.

I begged Him to take my life and to assure me that He would welcome me home to heaven. I longed to be with Him. I only had one thought and one question left, and that was "what does it feel like to die?"

One evening, after about three and a half months of torture, as I was just waiting to experience death, one of the soldiers came to the door and called my name. It was just as they had done before each of the previous executions that they had shown us in those newspapers. Usually, they would call more than one name, but this evening, only my name was called.

I struggled to reach the door, and by the time I got to it, the soldier locked the door and left. I wondered why he wouldn't wait or say anything. But I conceded that he was identifying me, so that he knew whom he was supposed to kill that night. But that night, no one came for me.

The next day, the same thing happened again. I heard steps nearing our door, a gun was cocked, and the door opened. My name was called and I struggled to get to the door. The soldier closed the door and walked away. Only this time, after the soldier had walked away, I heard a voice. He called my name, and said, "Today, before dawn, you will be out of this place." I announced to the room that I had heard a voice, but most of the men thought that I must be crazy. In the same way as one older man had also been hearing voices and seeing things until he went crazy, stepping on us and trying to run away and then finally dying. But my eyes were sober and my cousin-brothers asked me what the voice had told me.

I told them that, "I would be out of this place before dawn", and they asked me what that meant. I could only assume that it meant that of the three of us, I would be the first to die.

I also felt assured that God had heard my cry and that He was assuring me that I would be going home to heaven and would be welcomed by Him.

I eagerly awaited death. And sure enough, before dawn, at around 2 am, a soldier walked towards our cell. Cocking his gun, he called my name. As I struggled to the door, I turned around and glanced one last time at my cousins, saying good-bye with my eyes, knowing that I would never see them again.

As I walked down the hall, with a gun to my back, I awaited the feeling of a bullet entering my body. I closed my eyes a few times, expecting to be shot at any minute. I would take a few steps and then stop, thinking that the soldier would shoot me, but he would shove me from behind and tell me to keep on walking. I couldn't understand why he wouldn't just shoot me there.

I was led into a living room. Still waiting to feel death, I was told to pick a shirt from the pile of bloody clothes in the middle of the room. I chose a green-khaki shirt that was hard with dried, clotted blood. I unrumpled it, as dried blood fell on the floor. And I put it on. Then he motioned me to go see the man behind a desk in the corner.

As I sat there, the words that were spoken to me did not make any sense and I continued to expect a bullet in my head, even though I was hearing words of apology.

I was told what I already knew - that I had been falsely accused and that I had been arrested before any investigations had taken place. I was told that I was going home and that my cousins would follow, but that their wounds needed more time to "heal" before they could be released.

I was in shock and honestly didn't want to be released. I wanted to go home to heaven. I was convinced that the voice I had heard was telling me that I would be out of here – out of this world. I couldn't comprehend what was happening and rather than feeling relief or joy at being sent home, I was confused and disappointed. I wanted to die and still awaited the feeling of that bullet, which would end my life.

What was I being sent home to do? I had completely died to this life and had no ambitions or hopes or dreams. All I wanted was to be with God in heaven. Everything was settled between me and God, no stoned was left un-turned; I was ready to go.

I was brought to a vehicle, and shoved in, along with two other young men, including Junior (the 14 year old brother-in-law to my cousin). Before that moment, I hadn't known where Junior was. We hadn't seen him since that one day when he was interrogated in front of us. I found out that he had remained in a juvenile-cell, for about two months. He was released with me.

We were made to lean forward with our heads between our knees. A rifle was cocked and then placed on our necks, and we were told to balance it and not to move. We were driven to a local police station and told to wait there on the patio until the sun came up a few hours later. The police were told to keep us there until the morning when we could arrange to meet our families and go home.

One young man was met there by his Toto who had been searching for him. She brought him bananas and soda and offered me a banana to eat as well. Accepting that banana was a huge mistake. I had not needed to use the toilet for about a week and eating that banana caused extreme stomach pain; it was the worst pain that I had ever experienced, even after being tortured for over three months. I curled up on the patio and longed for rest. The rain falling on the tin roof and running down the side of the patio was no longer heard or felt, as the pain that I was suffering consumed my mind.

In the morning, instead of the police helping us to make a telephone call to find our family or to call a taxi to go home, the new police officers on duty decided it would be in their best interest to lock us up and demand bail. Only my family had no idea where I was, to come and pay for our release.

I was locked into a cell with criminals, who all assumed that I was newly arrested and must have managed to smuggle money in. They demanded that I give them money, to which I replied, "Do you have any idea where I have come from? Here you are given food and water…"

They forced me to stand with my hands in my pockets, between two men who had a competition to see who could slap me the hardest. One man would slap me and I would fall back and be caught by another man, who would then show that he could slap me harder, until I could not stand any longer. I was unable to open my mouth properly for about six months, and to this day, when I open my mouth wide to yawn, my jaw cracks.

Every time that the officer on duty walked by or came to find someone being brought before a judge, I begged him to please let me use his mobile phone. Finally, he allowed me out of the cell and told me to take a jerry can and fill a drum with water. He had left his phone out by the drum of water and told me to phone my family while fetching the water.

Thank God, He gave me a good memory for numbers! I was able to call my cousin-brother's in-laws and after a few hours, my brother's *Amuran* (Ateso for mother-in-law) came to pick me, and Junior, up. It was then that I realised that I was not very far from home, but with the pain that I felt and the fact that I could not stand up straight, I was unable to walk home. I took about 20 steps being the most steps I had taken in over 3 months and then sat down on the ground.

She called a taxi for us and brought me back to the house where we had been arrested months before. Junior went to be with his family.

The house had been destroyed and was just a shell. There were no doors or windows, and they had taken anything of value and destroyed what was left. Even my photo albums were gone. Every piece of furniture was cut open and turned upside down. The neighbours begged me not to sleep there, fearing that the same men who had taken me before would come back for me now. I assured them that I had not escaped but had been released and that if they had wanted to kill me, they had had every opportunity. Some neighbours moved the furniture aside so that I could lie down to sleep, and I rested until the next day.

My cousin wives and children had left and were fearful of coming back. They had all been traumatised by our arrest and were sure that we would be killed. I was brought food however, and taken care of as I began to heal.

17
SCARS

For though he wounds, he also bandages.
He strikes, but his hands also heal.

Job 5:18

Dear friends, never take revenge. Leave that to the righteous anger of God. For the Scriptures say,
"I will take revenge;
I will pay them back,"
says the Lord.

Romans 12:19

Examine yourselves to see if your faith is genuine. Test yourselves. Surely you know that Jesus Christ is among you; if not, you have failed the test of genuine faith. As you test yourselves, I hope you will recognize that we have not failed the test of apostolic authority.

We pray to God that you will not do what is wrong by refusing our correction. I hope we won't need to demonstrate our authority when we arrive. Do the right thing before we come—even if that makes it look like we have failed to demonstrate our authority. For we cannot oppose the truth, but must always stand for the truth. We are glad to seem weak if it helps show that you are actually strong. We pray that you will become mature.

2 Corinthians 13:5-9

IT WASN'T UNTIL SIX MONTHS later that my cousins were also released. They had not remained to heal, but had undergone even more torture. Another form of torture that they endured was to stand for hours in drums of water, falling or sitting would result in drowning.

Their bodies were covered with fresh wounds, while mine was forming scars – my back has several large keloid scars and I have a long scar on my neck from the whip - and my arms still had white lines from the ropes, as my skin was healing but hadn't become my brown skin tone yet.

When they were released, the military concluded their investigations and confirmed that all of this had happened because of the neighbour who lied, to get more land. He was also found with many of my cousin's things, including his vehicle. He wanted 500, 000 Ugandan shillings before giving the vehicle back, and my cousin was offered help from the military in making the payment. They said that they would give him the money, and he could arrange to hand the money over, so that they could arrest the neighbour, and we would never see him again. My cousin refused. He did not want to take vengeance, nor validify any ill feeling towards himself or his people.

With my cousin, Simon in 2015

After Robert and Simon were released our friends and family organized a celebration and I was asked to be the Master of Ceremonies. There were government officials invited and one woman, a Parish Chief, turned to me and said, "I can see the scars, but I can never know the pain, but the only way for you to move forward is if you forgive."

In disbelief, I screamed inside that she did not know what she was asking, and with tears of anger and bitterness streaming down my face, I dropped the microphone and walked off of the stage. That was the end of the party for me.

While I was a believer and was assured of my salvation and knew that God had saved me, not only from my sins, but out of the hell of that torture, I somehow shut down and didn't know how to go on living. I had been so convinced that God was going to bring me home to be with Himself, when I heard His voice in that torture chamber, that now I was confused about why I was still alive, and what I was supposed to do with my life. I had not only been prepared to die, but I didn't want to live this life, here on earth.

I tried to go on living by helping Robert and Simon, and by staying involved in church ministry. We also continued with the Slum Women and Children's Association.

I had used the rest of my Red Cross savings to help my nephews, caring for them for the six months while their papas were still in torture chambers. I thought that maybe I could study on my own and try to pass the accounting exams. And a friend gave me money to help with some of the fees.

I went to the local Kampala library, which by world standards wasn't much of a library. There was no Internet and I had access to only a few books that were out-of-date. But I studied as hard as I could.

When it came time for the exam, I failed.

I still didn't know why God had saved me and what I was supposed to do with my life now. I wished to continue my studies or to do business of some kind, but had no means and all of my old ambitions had died. I had died to myself and to this life, but hadn't yet learned what it means, as the Apostle Paul says, "to live is Christ".

I had no money, business, very little employment, and felt no purpose. I also had a difficult time making conversation with anyone and I suffered from flashbacks. My flashbacks didn't only take me back to those torture chambers, but to the battlefield where I grew up.

It could be in the middle of the day or in the dark of night. I would hear and see and smell the very real scenes around me and have a mind to cry out to God for help and to come up with a plan of escape. Then, when I was interrupted or "awakened," I would be confused, but still be able to recall the "dream" that I'd just had and convince myself that I was okay.

One day, I was with my nephew Jude when I heard the battle raging outside. I could hear AK47s firing nearby. People were running and screaming all around our house.

"Jude, get down!" I instructed my nephew.

"Uncle, what is wrong?" Jude asked, with a mix of fear and confusion on his face.

"They are coming, but it will be okay. Just stay down."

I assured him that I would protect him; that God was with us and would help us.

I planned an escape route, deciding that if the soldiers stormed the door, it would be safest to be in the middle of the floor. I planned out the distance from the door that I needed to be, so that I could get up and run under them to escape.

I eventually fell asleep; battling in prayer and waiting for the door to be knocked down in attack. I peed on myself and woke up confused but still in a defence mode.

"Uncle, what's wrong?"

"What's wrong?" I responded.

"What's wrong?"

And then I was back to reality. I always repeated the question of "What's wrong?" or "What's happening?" or "Are you okay?" and then would *wake up*. My nephew told me what had happened and he wondered what was wrong with me.

In my conscious mind too, I had allowed my mind to meditate on the horrors of torture. Only it wasn't a flashback. I was thinking of ways that I could take revenge and torture the man who had arranged our arrest.

If thoughts were to come true, I would have annihilated an entire tribe. But, in actual fact, God does tell us, in His Word, that we cannot claim to love God and hold hatred in our heart towards a brother, and that the sins of the heart are equal to physically sinning; to lust is to commit adultery, and to hate is to commit murder. I began to even find comfort in those thoughts, completely searing my conscience, and deceiving myself into thinking that I was living the life of a Christian.

I had been freed from that cell, but I was not living as a free man, I was choosing to live as if I was back in that safe house; becoming bitter and in bondage, while no longer tied.

PART TWO

Let all that I am praise the Lord;
with my whole heart, I will praise his holy name.
Let all that I am praise the Lord;
may I never forget the good things he does for me.
He forgives all my sins
and heals all my diseases.
He redeems me from death
and crowns me with love and tender mercies.
He fills my life with good things.
My youth is renewed like the eagle's!

Psalm 103:1-5

18
INTERVIEWED BY MY FUTURE WIFE

Furthermore, because we are united with Christ, we have received an inheritance from God, for he chose us in advance, and he makes everything work out according to his plan.

Ephesians 1:11

You can make many plans,
but the Lord's purpose will prevail.

Proverbs 19:21

I WENT HOME TO THE village a couple of times during that next year. During one visit, I borrowed a friend's motorbike and was speeding down a dirt road, just like I had with the Red Cross. Only this time I had no emergency relief to bring, and no need to be travelling at 120km/hr.

I had no way of knowing that just ahead, was a small herd of cows, being driven by a young boy. A boy was driving the cattle from the garden and as he was hitting them, the cattle came running and one bull jump to the road, and I met it in the moment it joined the road.

I couldn't break or swerve, but hit it straight on at 120km/hr. I flew with the bike. It clipped my ankle and then fell to one side as I continued to fly through the air. When I landed, I slid for several feet in the grass and dirt, before finally stopping.

Villagers came running to my aid, but I was in shock and thought that I could get up and continue riding. They urged me to stop and brought me to a clinic, but the nurse took one look at my torn-up knee and went into shock herself. She had to go out and vomit and couldn't even treat me so I had to treat myself.

After removing the small stones that were embedded in my flesh, mostly on my right knee, I bandaged myself up, asked for the motorbike and continued on my way. Once home, I was able to rest and recover.

I was back in the village for Christmas 2003. It had been a year and half year since my arrest and torture, and I was searching for a purpose to my deliverance.

During a visit to Soroti Town in January 2004, I met up with an old friend from school. He told me that he had heard something on the radio that I might be interested in. He said that there were interviews being held on Market Street. He walked with me, warning me to make sure that I didn't have to pay for the application form because it could be a scam. It was common to charge for the application and then not even have a job opening.

We arrived to ask for applications and to find out more information. We saw a little room set up for interviews. There were two Iteso – fellow tribesmen, and three Mzungus, a man and two young women who looked like twins.

Charity, organising application forms, 2004

The name of the organization was New Hope Uganda (NHU). One of them explained that they were looking for prospective staff members for a new Christian children's centre that would be established in my district to provide for the fatherless and for child soldiers who had escaped from Kony's army. At the time, there were internally displaced people everywhere. People had fled to Soroti and were setting up war camps, similar to the ones where I had grown up. And there was a problem with children needing refuge because they were at risk of being abducted into the rebel army. I thought that maybe I would find purpose in serving at a children's centre and decided to apply. I was given an application form and told to come back the next day for interviews.

Charity visiting internally displaced people camps in Soroti, in 2004

The next day, I was interviewed by two of the Mzungus: Tom and one of the girls. Later, I was told that I'd passed the preliminary interviews and to be ready to head to Luweero, with the other candidates, for a conference to learn the theological foundation for the ministry of New Hope Uganda and to learn more about their vision and mission. We were told that we would also have further interviews. While there I was given a scholarship to their training institute.

(left to right) Tom, Charity, Kokus, Shadrach and Adrienne)

I was chosen, along with three others from Soroti, to take the course at their training institute, with practicum at their local Christian children's centre and school. Also enrolled were Ugandans from different tribes (including a Ugandan-Indian), three Kenyans, two Americans and a Canadian. The Canadian girl was named Charity, the same girl who had interviewed me in Soroti. I didn't know it yet, that Charity would later become my wife.

19
FREEDOM IN FORGIVENESS

"You have heard that our ancestors were told, 'You must not murder. If you commit murder, you are subject to judgment.' But I say, if you are even angry with someone, you are subject to judgment! If you call someone an idiot, you are in danger of being brought before the court. And if you curse someone, you are in danger of the fires of hell.

"So if you are presenting a sacrifice at the altar in the Temple and you suddenly remember that someone has something against you, leave your sacrifice there at the altar. Go and be reconciled to that person. Then come and offer your sacrifice to God..."

Words of Jesus Matthew 5:21-24

"If you forgive those who sin against you, your heavenly Father will forgive you. But if you refuse to forgive others, your Father will not forgive your sins..."

Words of Jesus in Matthew 6: 14, 15

DURING THE FIRST DAYS AT the Institute, New Hope Uganda began a National Reconciliation Campaign, calling for tribes to come together and repent of the past atrocities committed by their fellow tribesmen against other tribes and to be reconciled one tribe to the other. As a class, we joined them by interceding for the reconciliation of Uganda.

In our first night of intercession, I was asked to lead the evening and as we gathered together to pray, I heard a voice saying, "You must begin with yourself." I turned to look behind me, thinking it was a joke. But no one stood there.

I quickly defended myself in my mind though. I responded by questioning why I would need to begin with myself. I held no bitterness or unforgivingness in my heart towards any other tribe, or towards any individual - or so I had convinced myself.

Just then, I saw, like a slide show, the celebration after my cousins had been released from torture. I saw the Parish Chief lady standing in front of me and her statement to me " I can see the scars but I cannot comprehend the pain yet the only way for you to live past your scars is if you forgive" and me dropping the microphone and walking away from the party. During this moment the holy spirit brought me face to face with the condition of my heart, my unforgiveness, anger and bitterness. I saw myself drop the microphone and walk off the stage. Then I felt a fresh chocking wave of bitterness in my heart toward those who tortured me and toward the man who orchestrated it.

I broke down and began to cry. Some pastors and leaders came around me to pray for me and ask what was wrong.

I wept and shared, for the first time, about my arrest and torture and about my hatred and fear. The Ugandan military speaks Swahili, so it was the language of the soldiers that I knew as killers, growing up and also the language of my torturers. *(I can completely understand Swahili, but cannot speak it, as I have a mental block).*

It was the first time that I had wept over what I had experienced, but

I was also weeping for the sin of unforgivingness and bitterness in my heart. I could taste the bitterness, like bile, as I cried and prayed and struggled to forgive. The pastors and my new classmates prayed for me and encouraged me to "let it go".

I had been holding onto unforgivingness and keeping my torturers imprisoned in my mind. I was allowing unforgivingness and hatred to control me.

When I finally let it go, when I chose forgiveness, I felt such freedom. I also experienced immediate healing in my mind. I was completely set free of the flashbacks that had become part of my life.

20
LESSONS FOR LIVING

By his divine power, God has given us everything we need for living a godly life. We have received all of this by coming to know him, the one who called us to himself by means of his marvelous glory and excellence. And because of his glory and excellence, he has given us great and precious promises. These are the promises that enable you to share his divine nature and escape the world's corruption caused by human desires.

In view of all this, make every effort to respond to God's promises. Supplement your faith with a generous provision of moral excellence, and moral excellence with knowledge, and knowledge with self-control, and self-control with patient endurance, and patient endurance with godliness, and godliness with brotherly affection, and brotherly affection with love for everyone.

The more you grow like this, the more productive and useful you will be in your knowledge of our Lord Jesus Christ. But those who fail to develop in this way are shortsighted or blind, forgetting that they have been cleansed from their old sins.

So, dear brothers and sisters, work hard to prove that you really are among those God has called and chosen. Do these things, and you will never fall away. Then God will give you a grand entrance into the eternal Kingdom of our Lord and Savior Jesus Christ.

2 Peter 1:3-11

FOR THE NEXT FIVE MONTHS, I studied at the Institute, which was like an intense Bible School. We enjoyed lectures in childcare, biblical counselling, biblical family and marriage, Christian education, biblical management, accounting and much more. There was also a practicum at NHU. We learnt how to establish and manage a Christian children's centre and school.

After graduation, I was asked to stay on to work in the Accounts department, because the centre in Soroti was not yet ready to be established. I had the opportunity to continue learning in a Christian community, where we related as family and referred to each other as auntie and uncle. I was also given the privilege of teaching on biblical management at the Institute.

(Me) teaching biblical business management at NHICF

I worked in the Accounts department, but was also involved in the children's centre community. I was able to earn a steady income, and invested some of it into a business in Kampala. I also sent my sister Jemimah through school, using my new income and she eventually graduated as a nurse.

The business in Kampala was a printing business. I rented an office space where all of the other photocopy and print business were. I had a friend who partnered with me. He took care of things while I was still at the children's centre and institute. We advertised a competitive price, did all of the design work, but then brought the final product for printing at another shop, while saving up to purchase our own machines. By the time we had raised enough money to advance our business, my "friend" disappeared with all the money.

I couldn't understand why God wasn't blessing my business venture. But he was providing for my needs and was teaching me and bringing more and more change to my heart. He was slowly bringing healing from all of my past adversities.

While I had been completely healed of all of the flashbacks, in the instant of forgiving, I still struggled with being sensitive to sounds in my sleep. Because of the sleep torture that I had endured, I was always on alert, even in the deepest sleep. I could sleep, but could not rest.

I could be in what I felt like a deep sleep when my roommate would come to the door and before his hand was on the doorknob, I was at the door. I could wake up, get up and run across a room in a split-second. God wouldn't bring healing in that area of my life until after I was married 4 years later.

I lived, worked, and learned at this children's centre and Church community from January 2004 until September 2005. God used that time to mature me in my walk with Himself and also to give me a glimpse of the vision and purpose of my life.

Charity and I with our graduating class of 2004 at NHICF

During this time, I made many life-long friendships. I received amazing insight and encouragement from people like the Herskowitz family, the Shoracks, Auntie Constance Dobbs, Uncle Shadrach and Auntie Sarah Okiror, the McFarlands, Ann Imusatlaba, Kokus Otim and the Ebenezer family (which I was part of for two years). I was also blessed to know and learn from the Bakimi and Dangers families, who founded the beautiful ministry of NHU, which seeks to bring the Fatherhood of God to the fatherless through family structures, Christian education, and biblical self-sustainability.

21
A FATHER TO THE FATHERLESS

*Father to the fatherless, defender of widows—
this is God, whose dwelling is holy. God places the lonely in families*

Psalm 68:5, 6a

IN SEPTEMBER 2004, I WENT for a walk to Hope House, a baby house where orphaned and abandoned babies were cared for. While I had been studying and working at New Hope Uganda for nine months, I had never visited the baby house.

I knew, as soon as I set eyes on a particular baby boy, that he was supposed to be my son. I felt God's Father-heart well up inside of me, unlike anything I had ever felt before. I felt in that instant that this is what my life was spared for. This is why God freed me from those torture chambers. He saved me to take care of this baby.

I had probably thought about getting married one day and having children, but had never imagined this feeling. I wanted to take him home that very day. Of course, I wasn't allowed to, but when the sincerity of my request was seen, I was instructed on what steps to take to prepare for being a foster-father. He was around three months old.

I visited him every day. I changed his nappies (diapers), gave him his bottle and got him to sleep every night. I did everything needed to prepare myself and my hut at the Institute for having a baby. And for Christmas that year, I was given the gift of a son.

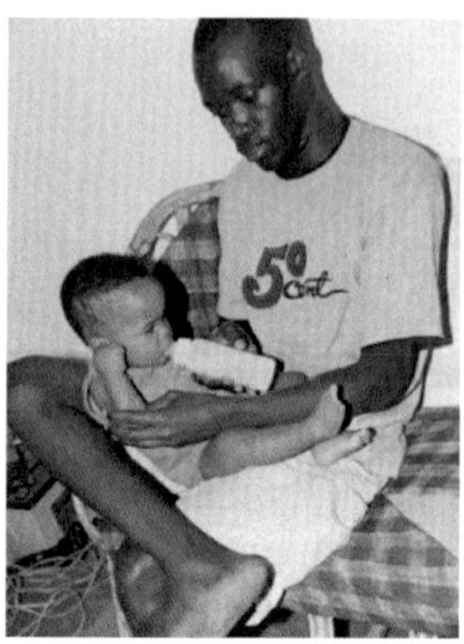

I named him Benjamin Eseuna. Benjamin means, "son of my right hand", and Eseuna is a word in my mother-tongue, meaning, "chosen one". I loved him as if he was my own flesh and blood – maybe even more. I loved him with the love of my Father-God, as He showed me how to love and brought even more healing to my heart and mind in caring for this baby.

As I watched Benjamin grow, I knew that I wanted to adopt him and make him my own son. But in the summer of 2005, I was forced to make one of the most difficult decisions of my life.

Amidst the oasis of personal growth and beautiful Christian fellowship, I encountered a problem with the Ministry Administrator, my superior in the accounts department. He instructed me to borrow funds from the safe, to make a payment, and he was to reimburse the funds as soon as possible. However, by the time the "borrowed" funds were needed, they had not yet been replaced. But instead of owning up to his decision, my superior told the leadership that he knew nothing of the transaction and blamed me for spending the said funds.

I was able to provide the necessary paper trail, including our written comments on the requisition. However, there was never any acknowledgement of me being falsely accused nor any apology. I forgave him, but I feared for what could happen in the future if such a scenario were to be repeated, especially if I didn't have the same written proof. In Uganda, it is not uncommon for someone accused of such a crime to be arrested and sent to prison. I felt like I had no option and that God was leading me to tender my resignation. I was then asked to remain in my position and even offered a raise, but I knew in the core of my being that this season of my life was over.

As soon as I tendered my resignation, I made a call to Habitat for Humanity Uganda. Back in 2003, after God had saved me out of that cell, I had gotten a job with someone who was creating a database of Ugandan non-profits, and had brought him around the country to meet with different directors. During that time, I became acquainted with the director of Habitat for Humanity Uganda, Matthew Robertson. In God's perfect timing, an internal job opportunity had just come up, and he already had my resume on file. He told me to come for an interview, in which I would need to be tested in my knowledge of Excel. Tom Herskowitz, at New Hope, had taught me some time-saving shortcuts and tricks, to use Excel more efficiently; I passed the test and was offered to begin work the very next week.

I didn't know that when I resigned, my fostering would also come to an end. I assumed that I would continue the process of adopting Benjamin as I moved to Kampala to work. But, I wasn't aware of the policy of Hope House. I needed to be an employee to continue foster care and I needed to be married in order to adopt. I still chose to leave, and to entrust Benjamin into God's hands.

It was one of the most difficult decisions that I have ever made. Looking back, I can see that I never would have obeyed the call of God to leave Uganda, if I had decided to stay there. I thought that I was supposed to adopt Benjamin an d that he was the sole reason for God rescuing me out of that cell. How could I leave him behind? He knew me as his father and it felt so wrong to bring him back to the baby house and to say good bye. He was 14 months old. I felt as if my heart had been torn in two. And for the next year I suffered with nightmares of him being torn from my arms, kidnapped and abandoned, over and over again. He needed a father and I had left him.

Benjamin was later adopted by a wonderful Ugandan family at New Hope. God truly is a Father to the fatherless and sets the lonely into family. Ultimately God is Benjamin's Father and also his Comforter and Healer. I prayed for Benjamin every day for years and still remember him in my prayers.

God showed me that Benjamin was my foster son for a season, but it was not only for one Benjamin that He had spared my life. There are so many *Benjamins* out there, and God had a greater vision in mind than I could ever have imagined. When I had first felt that father-heart of love well up inside of my heart, it was only a glimpse of the heart and the burden that God would give me for the fatherless.

22
HABITAT

Work willingly at whatever you do, as though you were working for the Lord rather than for people. Remember that the Lord will give you an inheritance as your reward, and that the Master you are serving is Christ.

Colossians 3:23, 24

ON THE FIRST OF SEPTEMBER, 2005, I began work with Habitat for Humanity Uganda as an accountant for the USAID-funded Orphaned and Vulnerable Children (OVC) project. I worked in this position as a project accountant for six months.

With my Habitat shirt

While in this position, I saw transactions that didn't make sense to me. Once, I was looking at a receipt for goods from one of our projects, and there wasn't anything obviously wrong with it, my hair stood up, and I felt like there was something wrong. When I called the man who wrote and submitted the receipts to ask for an explanation, he said it was a mistake but couldn't explain what the mistake was. Then my Operations Manager came into the room and took the phone from me. He spoke for a moment and then hung up and turned to me. He seemed to have a better explanation for the receipt than the man who provided it. This raised my suspicions. I wondered how my superior could better explain a receipt from hardware store from hundreds of kilometres away, when the man who presented the receipt could not.

After a lot of research and prayer, I uncovered an internal corruption that went from the project level to the national office, (involving the operations and finance managers - both local staff). I sent my findings to the African Regional Office in South Africa.

When Habitat International came to do an audit, I was asked to come along with them to the field and to explain my findings. I was given no information but told to pack a bag for two weeks and that I would be given information when we arrived at our destination. We investigated *ghost houses* (houses that existed on paper only), and other forms of corruption. The entire organization had to be remade and was stripped down from over 35 employees to only 13 employees across the entire nation.

We worked hard together and I enjoyed the Christian fellowship and camaraderie of working together with fellow staff members at Habitat. I became close friends with a few colleagues. I was very blessed by our National Director Scott Metzel and by Ronald Ongopa, Collin Semakula and Mrs. Okau, to name only a few of my friends whom I enjoyed work and Christian fellowship with.

Another 8 months later I was promoted to National Accountant. As National Accountant, I worked in this position for almost two years before I was promoted to National Loan Portfolio Manager.

I continued to find corruption and would make citizen arrests with our driver Timothy.

I worked with our chauffeur to complete my work across the country. Sometimes, we would pick up project staff collector to show us a house that was behind in repayments. We had a secret code and on my word, Timothy would lock the doors (which could be controlled by the driver, so they couldn't unlock them). We would drive to the police station and I would go inside to make a report, providing all of the proof needed. When the police would tell me, as they often do in Uganda, that they would see what they could do, I would tell them that I had made the arrest for them and they only needed to come outside to arrest the culprit.

I was asked by Habitat International to speak at their International Management Conference in South Africa and enjoyed travelling there. We stayed in a hotel in the middle of a game park, surrounded by animals.

The signs said to keep your windows closed at night, but it was too hot, so I left my window open. In the morning, I woke up to find a baboon sitting at the end of my bed! Thankfully, he was more afraid of me than I was of him because baboons can be dangerous.

In my first conference in South Africa I thought that I had slept in and hurried to the restaurant for breakfast. Seeing only hotel staff, I thought that I had missed breakfast and was late for the conference. I was assured by the hotel staff though that I was not yet on South African time and the sun came up earlier there. It was not yet five in the morning. This was my first experience with time changes.

I was able to send my younger sisters to school and enjoyed fishing almost every day, when I was not travelling. I was enjoying life. God had also provided me with a godly friend and accountability partner in my colleague Ronald. We enjoyed running and praying together. I couldn't imagine life getting any better.

Ronny and I in a marathon

A little inlet of lake Victoria by the Habitat office in Kampala

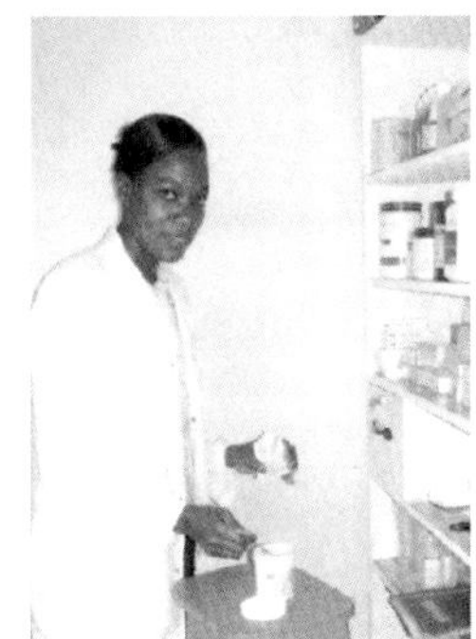

My sister Jemimah Alupo, working as a nurse

But before I could get too comfortable and settle into my old ambitions of making money and retiring early, God spoke to me. I wasn't made for this life. He hadn't saved me out of torture for this. I had already died to all of my ambitions. I had learnt to die to myself. Now I needed to learn to die a little bit more. I needed to choose to pick up my cross and to follow Him, even to the other side of the world.

Working at Habitat, living a very comfortable life, it may have seemed like a huge sacrifice to leave, but I knew that Christ had made the ultimate sacrifice and that I was to take up my cross and follow Him. I knew that if I could not leave Habitat and all of the ambitions that God had already stripped me of, that I was not worthy of the Gospel.

At the Institute, one of our required readings was a book by John Piper called, "*Let the Nations Be Glad!: The Supremacy of God in Missions*". In his book, Piper writes about the great missionary to Africa, David Livingstone (19 March 1813 – 1 May 1873), and the subject of sacrifice.

This is what Livingston said to Cambridge students about his leaving the benefits of England:

"For my own part, I have never ceased to rejoice that God has appointed me to

such an office. People talk of the sacrifice I have made in spending so much of my life in Africa. . . . Is that a sacrifice which brings its own blest reward in healthful activity, the consciousness of doing good, peace of mind, and a bright hope of a glorious destiny hereafter? Away with the word in such a view, and with such a thought! It is emphatically no sacrifice. Say rather it is a privilege. Anxiety, sickness, suffering, or danger, now and then, with a foregoing of the common conveniences and charities of this life, may make us pause, and cause the spirit to waver, and the soul to sink; but let this only be for a moment. All these are nothing when compared with the glory which shall be revealed in and for us. **I never made a sacrifice**."

I knew that ultimately it would not be a sacrifice. I know that in God's sovereignty I was meant to be working at Habitat and saving toward the mission field. It was a season and I still had more to learn about hearing God's voice.

23
A GENTLE WHISPER

"Go out and stand before me on the mountain," the Lord told him. And as Elijah stood there, the Lord passed by, and a mighty windstorm hit the mountain. It was such a terrible blast that the rocks were torn loose, but the Lord was not in the wind. After the wind there was an earthquake, but the Lord was not in the earthquake. [12] *And after the earthquake there was a fire, but the Lord was not in the fire. And after the fire there was the sound of a gentle whisper.*

1 Kings 19:11-12

God began to remind me of my love for the Spanish language that I had been introduced to while working with the Uganda Red Cross. He spoke to my heart about preparing to leave Uganda for the mission field. He began to show me that it was not only for one Benjamin that He had saved me.

When I had been working with Habitat for Humanity Uganda for a few months, I began praying for a wife. I had just left my foster son Benjamin, and I knew that if I had been married I could have adopted him. I had been told that if I wanted to keep him, then I had to remain and work there or get married. I knew that God was calling me to leave and I knew that I couldn't go ask someone to marry me so that I could adopt a baby. I didn't want my marriage to be based on my need for a mother for my adopted son.

Knowing that I would be going to the mission field, I began to save money and I began to pray for a wife. I wanted to be married and maybe even start a family before leaving Uganda.

One day in January 2006 as I was praying for a wife, I heard what sounded like an audible voice ask, "What about Charity?"

I responded almost incredulously, "What about Charity?"

I knew that the voice was referring to Charity Pilkey, the young lady who had interviewed me in Soroti two years earlier and who had been my classmate at the New Hope Institute of Childcare and Family.

"What about Charity?"

We were friends and kept in touch, writing e-mails every few months as an update on how we were doing. Charity was the one who introduced me to the Latin world. I had only known that people in Spain speak Spanish and had no idea of the need for missionaries in Latin America, where they also speak Spanish. In Latin America, there is a lot of *religion* but not many have been *discipled*. Also, the people and culture have been affected by war which, because of my own childhood, I can relate to.

I thought that maybe we would work together. She had been travelling to El Salvador, Central America since the year 2000 and had built relationships with the local church there. She had volunteered in government-run orphanages that cared for up to 50 babies in one room with only a few workers. She had told me of the need there and the opportunity to start a ministry for orphaned and abandoned children. But I had never thought of marrying her. How could I even say anything to her about pursuing a romantic relationship with her? She was on the other side of the world. I didn't even know where she was at the moment.

The very next morning as I logged into my computer at work, my yahoo account notified me that Charity was online. I had never seen her online before and we had never chatted before. I wondered if it was God or just a coincidence.

Charity was in Antigua, Guatemala, studying Spanish and was up late at an internet café, she also saw that I was online and decided to say hello.

I still wasn't convinced though. And I waited and prayed for the next seven months. But near the end of August 2006 I felt like God was showing me that He had already answered my prayer for a wife and I just needed to do something about it. I asked Him that if it was from Him that He would also say or do something to prepare Charity for my writing her.

On the other side of the world, back in Canada now, Charity didn't hear an audible voice, but the Holy Spirit was at work in her heart as well. She was helping her friend Amy prepare for her wedding. Amy had been to Uganda and they knew several of the same people. They were catching up and Amy asked about me. Although she had never met me, she had heard about me and Charity had told her of my interest in missions and the possibility of me serving in El Salvador. Amy asked Charity if she was interested in me as more than a friend. Charity replied no, that she loved me as a brother and really respected me and wanted to work with me in El Salvador. She had even thought that I could marry one of her El Salvadoran friends!

After the question though, she began thinking about me more and envisioning our working together in El Salvador. After one week she had come to the conclusion that she could *only* work with me if we were married.

It was God's perfect timing because the same day that Charity had concluded we should be married if we were to work together, I sent her an email. It had been several months since I had emailed about my work and asked her how she was doing. This e-mail was completely different though.

I didn't beat around the bush, as the saying goes. I let her know that I felt that it was God's will for us to get married and do missions together, beginning in El Salvador. I asked her if I could talk to her parents and ask their permission to court her with the purpose of marrying her. She said, "yes."

As with most of my life, courtship didn't come without challenges. I wanted to honour Charity's parents, and her own belief in God was that if it was His will then it would happen with the blessing of those she had submitted herself to. She wanted to honour her parents and they had never done anything like this before. Charity has five siblings, and at the time, only her sister Karissa was married. Karissa and Randy had *courted* as opposed to *dated*, and they were not an ocean apart. We submitted ourselves to the guidelines and boundaries that they set for our courtship and later for our engagement.

From September 2006 until April 2007, we enjoyed a long-distance courtship, with very strict guidelines. We could chat for one hour every Tuesday and could send and receive one email every Friday. After 8 months, we were finally allowed to talk on the phone, for one hour every last Saturday of the month.

It was also agreed that we could not become engaged unless I could travel to Canada and meet Charity's parents in person. I applied for a Canadian visa, but was denied because I didn't have sufficient travel history. I tried again after travelling to South Africa, but was again denied. I was denied three times and then requested that rather than meet in Canada, would Charity's parents travel to El Salvador? I knew that I was called to marry Charity and I knew that we were called to be in El Salvador, so it seemed like the perfect solution. They agreed and I began looking into how to get to El Salvador.

First, I would need a visa, but it must be easier to get than a Canadian visa, right?

I took my vacation leave from Habitat and travelled the 15 hours by bus to Nairobi, Kenya where more foreign embassies are. I had already discovered that there is no Salvadoran Embassy or Consulate in the entire continent of Africa, so I would first have to travel to another continent, where there was one. I stayed at a hotel for one week and applied for nine different visas to seven different countries, as I applied to Spain and France twice. I even had an invitation to visit brothers in Christ at a Youth With A Mission (YWAM) base in Spain, but that didn't help. By the end of nine days, I had used up a large percentage of my savings, paying for visas that I was never granted, and I finally gave up.

I had been asking for God to lead me, provide for me, and bless me in all of these applications. But He had been silent. Now, as I packed my bags and then sat on the bed, sobbing, questioning God and wondering if I had ever heard His voice in the first place, I again heard that same voice say,

"Stop crying."

"Get up. Go to the sixth floor in Life House building."

Without thinking or bringing anything with me, I got up. I wiped the tears from my face and walked to the Life House building. I knew that the Spanish Embassy was there, on the third floor. I had no idea what was on the sixth floor.

I got in the elevator and pressed number 6. As the elevator door opened and I stepped into a reception area, I saw the sign. I was in the Columbian Consulate. As I stepped through the door, the Columbian Consul himself stepped out of his office and greeted me.

I turned to look behind me, assuming that he was greeting someone else, even though I had ridden the elevator alone. But he ushered me into his office. We sat and talked, and even laughed. It was the first time that I had laughed in nine days. I was afraid that he thought I was someone else. But he didn't.

He told me to go back and get my passport and photos. Then he gave me his business card and told the receptionist to give me whatever visa I applied for when I came back. Then he left the Consulate.

God could not have been clearer. He had called me to El Salvador, and He had called me to marry Charity!

Now I only needed to find a flight route to El Salvador. That would use up most of the rest of my *missions* savings. It would take five days of travels, from Uganda to Kenya to South Africa to Brazil (where I spent 18 hours in the airport after I was denied boarding my next flight because airline staff mistakenly thought I needed a transit visa for Peru), to Peru to Columbia. In Columbia, I experienced a Spanish speaking country for the first time. I went through more trials and more miracles. And I was blessed to stay with the mother and brothers of friends from YWAM, El Salvador.

Then, with the Salvadoran visitor visa, I had to stop in Peru again. When I *finally* boarded the flight to El Salvador, it was like a dream. And, while flying, I fell asleep and had a dream that I was flying to El Salvador and sleeping, but when I woke up (in my dream), it was all just a dream! Thank God it was real, and then I landed in El Salvador, where Charity and I finally met again after 3 1/2 years. We had our first real date at a restaurant in San Salvador.

I stayed at a YWAM base and we spent 21 days touring the country, meeting church leaders, talking and dreaming together and of course meeting my future in-laws!

Charity's mom came down to El Salvador for one week and her dad came for a few days. They had already gotten several references and had a family friend interview me, but now they could ask me questions in person and get to know me as much as was possible in such a short time.

I had purchased a ring in the Nairobi Airport and was waiting for permission to finally and officially ask Charity to marry me. After a long interview with her dad, I went for a walk alone with Charity by the Pacific Ocean.

We got engaged by the Pacific Ocean and committed our lives and our relationship to the Lord as the waves crashed around us.

With Charity's mom, Lori Pilkey, touring El Salvador together, and getting to know each other

Charity's dad, Roy Pilkey, after giving permission for us to become engaged

Our engagement in El Salvador, November 27, 2007

We would have another four months apart and another denied Canadian visa before we would see each other again. Each time that we encountered a roadblock and each time that I was denied a visa, we were strengthened in our faith, but also received discouragement from those around us. Many family and friends concluded that if we were meant to be together then God would have provided the visa already. Others couldn't understand why we would honour Charity's parents and not just elope. People asked if we were supposed to be together then why not just go get married? If it was from God then why would it be so difficult?

24
BRIDE PRICE

"Here is Rebekah; take her and go. Yes, let her be the wife of your master's son, as the Lord has directed." When Abraham's servant heard their answer, he bowed down to the ground and worshiped the Lord. Then he brought out silver and gold jewelry and clothing and presented them to Rebekah. He also gave expensive presents to her brother and mother. Then they ate their meal, and the servant and the men with him stayed there overnight. But early the next morning, Abraham's servant said, "Send me back to my master."

Genesis 24:51-54

I HAD KNOWN IN 2005 that God was calling me to leave Uganda. And even before that, while working with the Red Cross, I knew that I wanted to work in a foreign country. But this season of my life lasted until March 2008 and in those last few months, I enjoyed my work so much that it was too difficult to resign. My friend Ronald asked me for months if I had put in my resignation yet. Even though my bride-to-be was coming and I knew in faith that God would provide the visa to Canada and we would be heading to El Salvador to begin a ministry to the fatherless, I still hadn't put in my resignation.

One day, I was meeting with my pastor, Josh Carlson of Calvary

Chapel Kampala, and he challenged me, saying, "either you didn't hear from God or you are disobeying His call." Finally, I obeyed and gave three months' notice. My last day of work with Habitat for Humanity Uganda was March 28, 2008, just after Charity had arrived in Uganda.

God provided us with a business to help take care of our needs and keep my sisters in school as well. And I purchased a loan portfolio from Habitat for Humanity after I had finally resigned. We later turned that business into a Microfinance business, providing loans to the economically active poor in Kampala, with a 100% repayment rate.

Charity and her sister Adrienne travelled to Uganda together to meet my family, and see the home where I grew up. Together we prepared for our introduction, which is a traditional wedding or public engagement in Uganda. I had been asked to provide a bride price, which is traditional in my culture, though not in Charity's. They wanted me to know how much they valued their daughter and if I would pay a bride price for a Ugandan bride then I should also pay a bride price for a Canadian bride. Part of the bride price was to provide my passport at our introduction, with a Canadian visa.

Introducing Charity to my family

Revisiting the office where we first met in 2004

We had researched and talked to several other missionaries and even some Canadian officials about what to do differently in applying for a Canadian visa. Even some officials had advised that it was impossible to get a visitor visa to Canada for the purpose of marrying a Canadian. We should get married first or come up with a different reason for visiting Canada.

We desired to honour Charity's parents about getting married in Canada and they didn't even want us to get married on paper before I could travel to Canada. We also knew that we couldn't lie and sin against God, so we purposed to prove the truth and provide as much information as possible about who we were, that our relationship and call to the mission field was legitimate, and that I would honour my visa.

Together, Adrienne, Charity and I travelled to Nairobi, Kenya. It was a long and turbulent 15-hour bus ride, through villages that had been burned down because of political turmoil. We were thrown around like rag dolls and felt more like passengers on a turbulent flight than a bus. The driver fearfully drove as fast as he could on bumpy dirt roads through villages that had been burned to the ground. Adrienne even hit her head on the ceiling and badly tore a fingernail. Charity's already bad back was worsened, and we prayed that our trip would be worth all of this pain.

At the Canadian Embassy, we presented a file about 5 inches thick. No exaggeration. We had to pass it under the security glass opening at the counter, in three batches to make it fit. We also presented Adrienne and Charity's passports to show that they had come all that way to apply in person.

While we waited at a nearby mall until we could find out about the visa interview, Charity's very frugal sister, Adrienne, bought us tickets to fly back to Uganda as none of us could fathom getting back on that bus for another crazy ride.

When we went back to the Canadian Embassy to get my interview time, I was told that I didn't need an interview, that I had been granted a 3-month visa!

With Ronald Ongopa, his wife Tina, and Collin Semakula, planning the introduction and watching a video message from Charity's family in Canada

Back in Uganda, on April 12, 2008, with help from family and friends, and using up the rest of my savings, we had an introduction.

Charity and I at our Introduction

Traditionally, an introduction is like a marriage ceremony, which introduces the bride and groom's families to each other and a bride price is paid, gifts given and sometimes other spiritual ceremonies are performed. It can also be like an engagement and the bride then goes with the groom's female family to prepare for the wedding day.

It is usually a time of fun and laughter and of sharing a meal together. The whole ceremony is a satire-like, theatrical event. Two tents are set up, facing each other, one for each family. And there is a smaller tent in the middle, where the Bride comes with her "maids" to greet everyone.

The groom's family arrives and requests to join the party. Each family has a "speaker" who does all of the talking on their behalf. The bride's speaker asked the groom's speaker why they have come to interrupt their party and the conversation goes back and forth, like a "stand-up-comedy" until the groom's family is finally welcomed in.

My family, joining the party

The groom is seated randomly on his family's side and one of the bride's *aunties* comes searching for a certain *guest* whom she knows. She pins a flower on his shirt and then amidst cheers and joyful ululating, the groom and his best man are lead to the seats of honour at the front of his tent.

Adrienne with the Pilkey Family Speaker, Collin (wearing a Mzungu shirt)

The speakers again, talk back and forth about why the groom has come and the girl that he is looking for. He is told that she is far away, in another village and that she needs *transport* (money) to bring her to the party. After he has provided an envelope (with sufficient money), the bride is brought to the middle tent (she walks or dances rhythmically to music, surrounded by bridesmaids). Once in the smaller, middle tent, she kneels with her maids to greet the groom's family.

Charity, her "auntie" Jane Sperling, and her maids, greeting the party

Then, one or more of the groom's aunties brings flowers to the girl that he chooses from the maids that are kneeling. The rest of the ceremony involves settling the bride price (which has already been decided on in a separate meeting) and then the groom's representative presents cows, animals and money to the bride's family. The family speakers also introduce each family member, hence the title, "Introduction". The bride comes to kneel and serve cake to the groom's parents. And everyone celebrates together with a meal.

We wanted to honour my family, but not conform completely to our culture (which often also includes superstitious ceremonies), so we prayed and discussed and planned a cultural and biblical fusion for our introduction. Using scripture as a code, our speakers or traditional family representatives would say what needed to happen next. We mostly used the biblical story of Isaac and Rebecca to give instructions about paying bride price and giving gifts to Charity's family.

Our Introduction was hosted by mutual friends, Chris and Jane Sperling in Jinja. Charity had known Chris from Church and School back in BC, and I had met them while working at New Hope. Chris is Canadian and Jane is Rwandese -Ugandan.

Charity and I with our man and maid of honour, Ronald and Adrienne

Chris and Jane had agreed to represent Charity's Canadian family, along with her sister Adrienne. And Chris' sister April and her family, as well as Jane's brother were also there. Adrienne had invited a few of her friends who also joined us, but traditionally, each tent or family side should be full of family coming to meet each other and to bless the union of the couple. We had invited several friends from the area of Luweero, where we had studied together, to come and celebrate with us and also to represent Charity's family. At the last minute, almost everyone cancelled! Some couldn't come because of the rains and bad roads and others had other last- minute plans or emergencies come up. My family had travelled all day the day before and stayed at a nearby hotel and we were all getting ready to go join the party. My tent was going to be full and Charity's tent was going to be almost empty, which would appear bad in my culture.

Jane and her brother Augustine, quickly ran around the village inviting whoever they could, to join to bride's side. They even had the brilliant idea of inviting the nuns of a nearby convent, who came to sit on Charity's family side and witness the party!

Chris Sperling, giving Charity to me in engagement, and praying for us

Charity was given to me in engagement by Chris and he prayed for us and committed our engagement and future to God. I presented Charity with her engagement ring (for a second time), a traditional monetary gift and my passport with the Canadian visa. The bride price was the equivalent of 8 cows, 7 goats and 1 lamb, as well as a gift for each of her family members - including a safari for my bride-to-be and her sister, which we enjoyed together at Queen Elizabeth National Park.

My brother Peter (in grey) with family representatives, bringing gifts for the Bride Price

As a little side-story here, one of our mutual friends and a colleague of mine from when we were both at New Hope, Francis Mugwanya, was unable to make it to our introduction. He asked if we could have lunch by Lake Victoria and catch up that way instead. While enjoying our whole fried tilapia fish and chips, he asked about how Charity and I came to be having an introduction. He had known us when we were at the Institute and were just friends. He had also known Adrienne, just as an acquaintance since one of her mission trips to

Uganda in 2000. He turned to Adrienne and said, "I guess we need to step-up our emailing". We all laughed and she definitely didn't agree to it at the time, but they were married in January 2010. Francis is the founder of Father's Heart Mobility Ministry and together, the Mugwanya family serve people living with disabilities in Uganda. And we have had the privilege of joining them on a couple of wheelchair distributions.

With Charity and Adrienne, visiting our friend Francis at Lake Victoria in April, 2008

We were able to spend some time with my home Church of Calvary Chapel Kampala and to share with the congregation about the vision that we had for El Salvador. Although they were not able to cover our expenses, they committed to covering us in prayer and they *sent* me, as the first Ugandan Missionary to El Salvador, along with my bride-to-be. Pastor Josh Carlson and his wife Natalie also planned to attend our wedding in Canada, which we were so thankful for.

At the end of April, we had to say goodbye again. Charity went ahead to Canada to plan our wedding with her mom, sister Karissa, and close friends. Back in November, we had already sent out "Save-the-Dates" in faith, for a June 7th wedding. I wrapped up things with our new business manager and with my family, and said goodbye before joining them in Canada, in May.

We knew that we would be together soon. And I knew that God would lead us and provide for us, but would not necessarily make it all easy. The struggle and the difficulty were for the testing of our faith. He would always work for our ultimate good and He would always work for His own glory!

We were married on June 7, 2008. Below are some photos of our wedding. Chris Sperling came from Uganda, and stood as my Best Man. Pastor Josh and Natalie from Calvary Chapel Kampala were also there to celebrate with us. And, God provided a mission organization, at our wedding, to send us as Agents and to provide a way for people to support us, as we left for the mission field with nothing but some wedding gifts.

Our wedding ceremony (and brief stand-up dessert reception), were held at Coastal Church, Vancouver, BC, Canada

Our bridal party with Charity's maternal grandparents

With some of our guests, including my pastor from Uganda

EPILOGUE

Dear brothers and sisters, when troubles of any kind come your way, consider it an opportunity for great joy. For you know that when your faith is tested, your endurance has a chance to grow. So let it grow, for when your endurance is fully developed, you will be perfect and complete, needing nothing.

If you need wisdom, ask our generous God, and he will give it to you. He will not rebuke you for asking. But when you ask him, be sure that your faith is in God alone. Do not waver, for a person with divided loyalty is as unsettled as a wave of the sea that is blown and tossed by the wind.

God blesses those who patiently endure testing and temptation. Afterward they will receive the crown of life that God has promised to those who love him.

But don't just listen to God's word. You must do what it says. Otherwise, you are only fooling yourselves.

… Pure and genuine religion in the sight of God the Father means caring for orphans and widows in their distress and refusing to let the world corrupt you.

Excerpts from James Chapter One

WHEN CHARITY AND I WERE married (06-07-08), God also began a new healing for me. I'd needed to warn Charity to never touch me when I was sleeping, but to always wake me up from a distance. I already knew, from the experience of having roommates, that if someone even touched a doorknob, it was as if they had touched me, and because of the sleep torture that I had endured, I would wake up with a rush of adrenaline; ready to defend myself by attacking the intruder before they attacked me.

After almost three weeks of marriage, and an amazing honeymoon in the Rocky Mountains of British Columbia, Charity came to wake me with our niece Lauren. She thought that I had heard her knocking and calling me. I was in a deep sleep and when she sat on the bed next to me I sat up quickly, with wide eyes and I almost hurt them. Charity turned it into a game with Lauren, who was almost two years old. For the next year, every time Lauren talked to me or about me, she exclaimed and used sign language to say, "Surprise, Uncle!"

A few months later in El Salvador, when God had given me the opportunity to share my testimony at Love and Hope Children's Home, a short-term missionary team member named Karen prayed for us and said that she believed that God would use Charity to bring a new healing to my body and that where being awakened suddenly had brought fear of pain, I would learn to wake up to a pure and loving touch instead.

God has done that. It wasn't sudden, but my mind has been completely healed. I am no longer on alert when sleeping, but can sleep in peace.

Some things that I didn't even realise I did, like when going out on a date with my wife, at the beginning of our marriage, I had to tell Charity where to sit and I had to be in the most advantageous seat in the café or restaurant. I needed to observe and be prepared in case of any threat; ready to protect and to escape. Now we can go out and enjoy conversation without me being on alert. The Lord has brought complete peace and as I keep my mind fixed on Him, He keeps me in His perfect peace.

It has been 9 years since Charity and I married and began a journey of faith together. We have been serving together in El Salvador, Central America since July 2008, three weeks after our wedding. We now have four beautiful children of our own, Benjamin Ezra Egiru (04-16-09), Eleanora Asire Lynn (05-31-11), Eseuna Samuel Eleazar (07-16-13) and Charity Alupo Leneah (03-01-15). We strive to teach them the Father-heart of God, and to train them up in the way that they should go.

Together we founded Fundación Corazón Del Padre in El Salvador (and The Father's Heart Foundation, USA and Canada). Our vision is to bring hope to the hopeless and to lead the *(spiritual and physical)* orphan to the Father-heart of God. Our mission is to place orphaned children into adoptive-style families within a sustainable community, caring for their holistic needs.

Receiving approval as a non-profit in El Salvador, with our son Benjamin

God has lead us, provided for us, protected us and also allowed us to face various, even life-threatening, trials as a family on the mission field.

As this book comes to an end, my life story does not. And, whatever the future holds, I know that God is good and will be with me through it all. May you also be encouraged. His mercies are new every morning. He sees the WHOLE story, from Creation to the ends of the age and into eternity. He loves you and has a plan for your life, a plan for your ultimate good and for His glory.

I pray that my testimony would encourage you to search to know God and to hear His voice through His Word and by His Holy Spirit, and above all, may you be encouraged to find freedom and healing in forgiveness.

We have learnt as a family the truth that all of the trials and pains of this life are but a shadow, which will make the light and glory of eternity so much greater *because* we have walked through them. May you also, no matter what the trial, fix your eyes on Jesus, He is the Light that has dawned on those living in darkness. Endure as Jesus endured the cross and then all will be made perfect in eternity with Him.

And, as a final testimony, when we began writing this story, my parents were not serving God, but now we praise God that they have both been born-again and are standing as a light in the spiritual darkness back home in our village. Papa has also come out of his depression and is finally beginning to rebuild the business that was destroyed over 30 years ago. Though he still struggles, he is now able to provide for his family, even in drought. Through their trials now, God is their Provider and Protector. May God continue to protect them and to use them for His glory, and may His Kingdom come and His will be done in the villages of Amuria. Please pray for them.

If you have not come to know Jesus Christ, as your personal Lord and Saviour; if you have not been born again, and are seeking to know who God is and what it means to be a Christian, please read more in the appendix.

AFTERWORD

By Charity Cherise Okurut

"Remove the heavy yoke of oppression.
Stop pointing your finger and spreading vicious rumors!
Feed the hungry, and help those in trouble.
Then your light will shine out from the darkness,
and the darkness around you will be as bright as noon.
The Lord will guide you continually, giving you water when you are dry
and restoring your strength. You will be like a well-watered garden,
like an ever-flowing spring. Some of you will rebuild the deserted ruins of your cities.
Then you will be known as a rebuilder of walls and a restorer of homes…"

Isaiah 58:9-12

THIS BOOK COULD NOT BE complete without writing about Fundación Corazón Del Padre, The Father's Heart Foundation, and the beautiful country of El Salvador. The above scripture was impressed on my heart for El Salvador in 2001, . The following *chapter* is about The Father's Heart Foundation. Following that, is my personal testimony - in brief. Pictured on the succeeding page, are our four children, and (some of) our Ugandan and Canadian family.

Our children

(most of) Our family

THE FATHER'S HEART FOUNDATION
A Ministry Overview

OUR VISION IS TO BRING hope to the hopeless, and to lead both spiritual and physical orphans to the Father-heart of God. Our mission is to place completely orphaned children into adoptive-style family with a godly couple who will care for their holistic needs and lead them to the Father-heart of God.

About El Salvador

Official Name: Republica de El Salvador
Form of Government: Republic
Capital: San Salvador
Population: 6,071,774
Official Languages: Spanish, Nahuatl
Area: 8,123 square miles (21,041 square kilometres)
Crops: Coffee, sugarcane, rice, maize, beans

Known As: The Land of Volcanoes. The smallest and most densely populated country in Central America, El Salvador is full of natural beauty.

History and Culture

Before the Spanish Conquest of 1524, El Salvador was made up of three indigenous states and was home to the Pipil, Chortis (a Mayan people dating back to 200 BC) and the Lencas. Even pre-conquest El Salvador was marked by war and the land divided by the "elite" royalty and traders. Human sacrifice was also commonplace.

When the Spaniards came, they brought Catholicism. Unlike the rest of Europe who had gone through the Reformation, Spain continued with the original traditions of the Catholic Church, discouraging common people from reading God's Word and from having a personal relationship with God as their Father. El Salvador became a Catholic nation and (by 2015), 50% are still Catholic, while about 40% identify themselves as Evangelical Christians. We have seen that there is a huge need for discipleship in the Salvadoran culture.

El Salvador gained Independence from Spain in 1821.

El Salvador's history is full of political conflicts because of the problem of land distribution. The early years of independence were ruled by an Oligarchy of elite land-owners, referred to as *the Fourteen Families*.

A Military Dictatorship (1931-1979) was followed by a brutal civil war (1980-1992) and since the *Peace Accords* and the deportation of Salvadorans illegally living in the USA, there has been a constant battle with *Maras* (gangs formed in L.A. during the war).

Natural disaster, poverty and violence contribute to generations of fatherless and completely orphaned children in El Salvador.

We have been serving alongside our growing family and God's people in an impoverished community in Quetzaltepeque, El Salvador since the Autumn of 2008.

Fundación Corazón Del Padre (The Father's Heart Foundation), was established as a non-profit in El Salvador in 2009. We are building relationships and sharing the Gospel in word and deed while we follow the government guidelines for being able to take care of orphans.

Our village is made up of large extended families. For generations, these families have been squatters, working in the nearby coffee and sugarcane plantations. Each family member has under $3.25 per day to cover all of their living needs.

Education is a struggle. Many families do not see the value in sending children to receive an education which they never needed themselves. They may reason that to pick coffee does not require reading and writing skills. Most families cannot afford to send their children to school, even though education is "free", as they cannot afford books, shoes and other supplies.

Another problem with education is that the public-school system obliges teachers to pass children from one grade to the next in primary school. Once a child is in 4th grade and cannot read, write or pass a math exam, they fail the grade. Most children drop out of school after 4th grade, between 11-14 years of age, putting them at risk with the gang. Girls commonly become mothers around the age of 13, and their common-law "husbands" may leave them widowed or abandoned (because of gang violence or imprisonment) at age 15.

A few families grow their own food or keep animals, but the majority of squatters are not allowed, by the land owners, to have a garden or even chickens. Living in poverty, regularly affected by natural disasters, like hurricanes and earthquakes and oppression, leaving many families feeling hopeless.

Our Mission

Our master plan includes a community centre where families can come for teaching, training, counselling and medical care. But even now, on a small scale, through Bible study, discipleship, sports, nutrition, clothing, improved housing and education, the Foundation reaches over 100 neighbouring families. It is our desire to bring hope to every neighbour and to see them come out of poverty and a life of fear and to live a life changed by the Gospel of Jesus Christ.

The Gospel brings HOPE. Christ offers Salvation and a hope for eternity. He also promises us every spiritual blessing and brings peace, joy, patience, faithfulness, gentleness, self-control, genuine love, forgiveness and the will to work for His glory. In His wisdom, God tells us that in this world we will have troubles, but He has overcome the world. He will bring complete restoration, healing and holiness at the end of time, but for now He offers glimmers of hope and he changes lives for His glory.

We believe that Jesus is the hope of the nations. We have been commanded to make disciples of all nations, baptising them and teaching them to observe all that Jesus commanded. We are also told in the book of James, that true religion is to take care of the orphan, widow and refugee and to live lives of holiness, separate from the world.

We have seen the changing power of the Gospel in our village in El Salvador. Just a few testimonies of lives touched are Manuel and Mare who have been lead to salvation. Manuel has been baptised, they are being discipled and have decided to sanctify their 50+ year long common-law-marriage. Manuel became blind in 2011 and was afraid for our lives. When we prayed for wisdom and for peace, God answered by opening Manuel's spiritual eyes to see angels surrounding and protecting us!

Another elderly couple, Vicente & Antonia and their granddaughter Ashley have been faithful members of our discipleship group since 2010. The Foundation provides for their needs by employing Vicente as a caretaker.

Maricela was abandoned by her mother as an infant and never knew her father. She has been able to receive the love of a father through the Foundation and we have also been sending her to school and helping her mom who came back to take care of her when she was nine.

In our neighbouring village, most of the families that we know, are women-lead and most children have experienced several "fathers". The “fathers” are often abusive and usually involved in crime; ending up in a prison cell or a grave. There is a cycle of abuse and neglect. This generation of fathers grew up during the war and were left abandoned or orphaned by their own fathers. Without intervention, their sons will most likely do the same and their daughters will look for love in *the wrong places.*

We are already intervening and teaching, by example and through discipleship, what it means to be a father - a godly father who models the Father-heart of God. The Foundation will continue to reach our neighbours and be an example to them as we set up adoptive-style families for children who are completely orphaned.

Sustainability

Charitable organisations around the world are known for having an "open hand"; in need of donor-based funds. Some organisations, much like the inactive poor of the world, use their need as an asset. We believe that aside from the initial donations needed to begin a grass-roots organisation, we should strive to be sustainable and not dependent on regular outside funds.

Our goal is to be 100% sustainable through agriculture and business. Our very first structure was built with funds which mostly came from an aquaponics venture. While we do need funds for the initial development, and construction of the children's centre, we will not be dependent on continued annual donations once the centre is fully operational.

The children's centre will also be fitted with aquaponics. Aquaponics combines greenhouse agriculture production and fish farming, to produce a complete meal, in year-round farming. We also have a small poultry farm and will eventually raise all of the food needed for the children's centre, ensuring that the children in our care have access to complete and nutritious meals as well as education in sustainable farming. Our target is to produce at least 800,000 pounds of food each year.

Rice, beans, and tortillas are the staple foods in El Salvador. Malnutrition is a leading cause of death among the poor rural people who cannot afford more than one (incomplete) meal each day. Monthly food costs are often higher than monthly house rental costs in El Salvador - it is vital that we have a programme to provide food to our centre and to teach our neighbours how to produce their own food.

Board of Directors and Ministry Partners

Since 2009 we have had a local board of directors in El Salvador, made up of Salvadorans, North Americans, Africans, Asians and Europeans. Construction of the much-needed exterior wall has mostly been financed through this board and constructed most by our local bricklayers foreign and some foreign teams.

In 2015, we were approved as a non-profit in the USA. Each USA board member has visited or lived in El Salvador and assists in networking and fundraising. The Father's Heart Foundation, Canada was approved in 2017 and we have a Canadian board who will assist in fundraising, sending teams and taking care of missionary care for our family and any other Canadian missionaries on furlough.

All of the work accomplished in our village so far, has been done by volunteers, working with local labourers. We thank God for each individual, family and team who has served alongside Fundación Corazón Del Padre from 2009 to date.

We have worked alongside over 50 international teams, the majority of which were shared, along with resources, food and clothing, by other Christian missions in El Salvador including: Amor y Esperanza, The Christian Mission Alliance, Mission to El Salvador and Youth With A Mission. We also work with fellow missionaries and other expats in El Salvador, as well as local high school teams and local Pastors. We have also hosted missionary nannies who have served alongside us and helped with housekeeping and childcare. And, we have taught several interns.

Each volunteer has something unique to offer and also takes home a unique experience and story to share with others. We love our Christian community in El Salvador and the fact that we work together and have fellowship together.

One Intern, David Music, served and studied with us for a few months in 2012 and then came back with his new bride, Marie, to manage the entire ministry for the year of 2015. We are so thankful for them, and for each person who has chosen to spend themselves on behalf of the needy.

How to Partner With Us

There are many ways to get involved with The Father's Heart Foundation. Below are a few examples.

Missionary Teams

We host short to mid-term individuals and teams. A team may be: high school, homeschool, church, business, family or friend groups of 2-22 people. If you would like to join or lead a short-term missionary team, we would love to host you and give you a variety of ways to serve. From teaching Bible lessons, doing community outreach, building or repairing a home for one of our neighbours, working in construction, farming and discipleship, teaching English and more.

Visitors will also have the opportunity to tour this beautiful country and experience things like hiking a volcano, visiting a coffee plantation, seeing Mayan ruins, spending a day at the beach and shopping at a local artisan market.

Sustainability Discipleship Farm

If you are passionate about discipling others and enjoy farming, this is for you. We train aquaponics enthusiasts, missionaries and other interest groups with a hands-on approach. While we invest in you, you will be expected to spend between 20 to 30 hours a week helping in the management of the gardens, which involves: planting, transplanting, harvesting, feeding the fish, chickens and quail, packaging and distribution of the produce. At the same time, you will be discipling two to five Salvadoran young people while you work in the garden.

Family, Childcare and Education

We need dedicated long-term and mid-term missionaries to serve in the childcare department as family leaders, biblical counsellors, teachers, tutors, housekeepers and extended family members.

Serve as a Board Member and Network on our Behalf

Each year, we elect or re-elect board members in El Salvador. We need godly men and women who can sit on our board of directors to guide the foundation, help with fundraising and networking and to keep us accountable in the work that God has called us to. If you are gifted at networking and do not feel called to sit on a board, we would still love to connect with you.

Pray

Pray for the Lord of the harvest to send out workers! Pray for God to be glorified in our lives and ministry, pray for our personal walks with the Lord to grow and to bear fruit, pray for provision, direction and safety, and pray for the children and families and nation of El Salvador, pray that God's Kingdom would come and His will would be done on this earth as it is in heaven.

Invest in Sustainability

Make a one-time or recurring financial gift, which will be invested in The Father's Heart Foundation to grow and keep on giving. We need funds for construction and for farming start-up.

For a current list of needs and an update on what stage of ministry we are at right now, please write to me at: the.okuruts@live.com. To follow our family blog, go to: www.theokuruts.blogspot.ca. You can also visit our website at www.fhfusa.org.

CHARITY'S TESTIMONY

But I will keep on hoping for your help;
I will praise you more and more.
I will tell everyone about your righteousness.
All day long I will proclaim your saving power,
though I am not skilled with words.
I will praise your mighty deeds, O Sovereign Lord.
I will tell everyone that you alone are just. O God,
you have taught me from my earliest childhood,
and I constantly tell others about the wonderful things you do.
Now that I am old and gray, do not abandon me, O God.
Let me proclaim your power to this new generation,
your mighty miracles to all who come after me.

Psalm 71:14-18

I WAS BORN IN SURREY, British Columbia, Canada, on May 3, 1981. I was the third of six children born to Roy and Lori Pilkey. My first crib was in the church nursery. My family was very involved in the church. I was led to pray with Mrs. Johnson, my Sunday school teacher at Bible Fellowship, when I was five years old. I knew that I needed Jesus to be my Saviour I asked Jesus to save me from my sins and to use me to *Go and Tell the Story (as the Sunday School song says).*

My childhood was a medley of joy and of pain. I find it easy to relate to those who grew up in the church and also to those who grew up in a broken family.

I have experienced several life-threatening events, sickness and accidents personally and in my family. Growing up, I often thought that God's blessing and love were not meant for me *personally*. Through it all though, I eventually learnt that God is good and His Word is true. He does work everything out for our good and for His glory. I have learnt the amazing power of forgiveness and of choosing to love with a first Corinthians love.

When I was 12, I felt God's love in the midst of pain and learnt personally, that God is my Father and that even if those who have taught me about God's Word are not faithful to live it out, that His Word is still truth and He is faithful.

I was baptized at the age of 14 and was equipped and involved in missions at home and abroad. I went on my first overseas mission trip with a high school team from The King's School in March 1996, to New Hope Uganda. In 1998, I went with a missions team to Eastern Europe and in January 2000, I travelled alone to serve with missionary friends in El Salvador. I volunteered in an institution for orphaned and abandoned children and was overwhelmed by the need, while helping in a small room with 50 babies and only a couple of workers. I then began going on regular missions trips to El Salvador, connecting with a local church there. I volunteered at different orphanages and served in Women's Ministry.

Even in employment, I was passionate about missions. I never had a desire to further my formal education towards a specific career. I wanted to be a career missionary. I always enjoyed reading, studying, researching and attending as many seminars and classes as I could, to train in theology, trauma counselling, and missions in general. I began working in childcare when I was only 10 years old, and maintained several long-term babysitting, nannying and housekeeping positions over the next 15 years. I was a caregiver for a little special needs boy and also to a woman with Alzheimers. I also had experience working with horses, at a family restaurant and as a wedding florist.

In 2004, God miraculously provided for me to attend the New Hope Institute of Childcare and Family in Uganda. My sister Adrienne and I travelled to Uganda one month before the Institute began, to travel around and to visit other friends and organisations. During that time, we were asked to serve on an interview panel that was going to Soroti, Uganda. Although I wouldn't realise it until years later, it was there that I met, and personally interviewed, my future husband.

At the Institute, I was encouraged and convinced of the truths that I had grown up with, and God also revealed new truths to me about His character, missions and His calling on my life. Near the end of the Institute, I nearly died of malaria and was confronted with the need to be ready to die - and to choose to die to myself daily. I also made many wonderful friends and became close to several Ugandans, including some of the children at New Hope, Jane Sperling, and Shadrach and Sarah Okiror. Sarah actually told Samuel, during the institute, that if he was looking for a wife, he should look at me (he was not looking at the time, but later remembered what Sarah said). Shadrach joined us in celebrating our introduction, and we have been back to visit them as a family.

When I got home, the church that I fellowshipped in encouraged me to find a missions organisation or other church to send me to El Salvador. They also discouraged me from serving as a single woman.

I had always wanted to experience the pure love and leadership of someone *over me,* whether a father, the church leadership, or a husband. I had never dated and had been content being single, and actually appalled at the idea of anyone even thinking that I was in a relationship with anyone. I wanted to have a brotherly relationship with all of the men in my life. Especially because of my past, I wished that everyone would see me as *pure*, and never question my integrity. I had several life-lessons in truly seeking the approval of God, and not of man; fighting against insecurity (and, I am still a work in progress). I wanted to be completely satisfied in Christ, whether married or single. I had learnt that God is the best Father and knew that He is ultimately the best Husband.

I did want to get married and have children *someday*, but with the burden of wanting to do missions in El Salvador and of having a vision beyond myself (for seeing a new children's centre established), I began to pray desperately for a husband. My deepest desire became to marry a godly man who would lead me to the mission field (anywhere). I wanted to be the helper of someone with a greater vision than I had been given; someone who loved God and faithfully lived out the Gospel.

God did indeed give me the deepest desire of my heart, in my husband! Through my marriage and through His Word, God has completely healed me of the effects of the childhood traumas that I thought had permanently made me damaged and ashamed. I am now passionate about seeing others find healing in the Gospel too. I am so thankful for a husband who does not hold to his culture, but strives to live according to God's Word. I have felt God's love through Samuel in a very tangible way, while also being encouraged to find everything I need in my Saviour, and not in my husband.

Today, through continual trials, which we strive to count as JOY, we continue to serve in El Salvador and to trust the God who called us, to provide. God has also blessed us with four beautiful children: Benjamin (2009), Eleanora (2011), Eseuna (2013) and Charity (2015). They are learning the truths of God's Word along with us, and learning by experience the truth that *this is not our home*. All of our relationships, the church, missions, and family life are a shadow of things to come.

Already in their young lives our children have experienced even life-threatening trials and testings of their faith. Together we look forward to a new Celestial City where all pain, tears, and sin will pass away, and all things shall be made new. And while we wait, we strive to bring Him glory, and we obey Him in making disciples.

It is my prayer that my children and all of the children who are or will be part of our larger Fundación Corazón Del Padre family, will have a real glimpse of the blessings, love and promises of God fulfilled *here* on earth, as it is in Heaven.

WHAT MUST I DO TO BE SAVED?

If you do not have a personal relationship with God, or do not believe in God at all, I implore you to seek the truth for yourself.
If you are seeking to know God, and want to know what it means to be "saved", and what you must do to be saved, then the best place to start is with God's Word (the Bible), and on your knees in prayer.

Through this book I have testified of the Lord's faithfulness amidst unspeakable despair, pain and torture to the point of death and yet the Lord heard my cry, saw my tears and swiftly came to my rescue and called me out of a high security torture chamber. I hope that this testimony will cause you to consider seeking the truth that is found ONLY in the Bible. I recommend that you start your reading from the Books of John, Hebrews and Romans. Some excerpts are below, but find a Bible and search for truth there.

You and I know that death is real - just as life is real, and evil is real, just as God is real. If you would like to explore more about faith and spirituality, please do not hesitate to contact me or reach out to the nearest Bible teaching Church near you.

As a family and ministry, we tend to stay away from *prefabricated prayers* or instructions for salvation. But, we do want to take the opportunity, for those who want to know, to share a few scriptures to answer the question, "what must I do to be saved?". Then, only you know the sin in your own heart and life, and can truly repent, and come to God in faith for Salvation – we cannot do it for you.

If you send us an email, we can help to connect you with a local church, answer any questions, and pray with you.

Below are some excerpts from The New Testament of the Holy

Bible, (NLT).

Hebrews 11:1-3

Faith shows the reality of what we hope for; it is the evidence of things we cannot see. Through their faith, the people in days of old earned a good reputation.

By faith we understand that the entire universe was formed at God's command, that what we now see did not come from anything that can be seen.

John 3:1-21

There was a man named Nicodemus, a Jewish religious leader who was a Pharisee. After dark one evening, he came to speak with Jesus. "Rabbi," he said, "we all know that God has sent you to teach us. Your miraculous signs are evidence that God is with you."

Jesus replied, "I tell you the truth, unless you are born again, you cannot see the Kingdom of God."

"What do you mean?" exclaimed Nicodemus. "How can an old man go back into his mother's womb and be born again?"

Jesus replied, "I assure you, no one can enter the Kingdom of God without being born of water and the Spirit. Humans can reproduce only human life, but the Holy Spirit gives birth to spiritual life. So don't be surprised when I say, 'You must be born again.' The wind blows wherever it wants. Just as you can hear the wind but can't tell where it comes from or where it is going, so you can't explain how people are born of the Spirit."

"How are these things possible?" Nicodemus asked.

Jesus replied, "You are a respected Jewish teacher, and yet you don't understand these things? I assure you, we tell you what we know and have seen, and yet you won't believe our testimony. But if you don't believe me when I tell you about earthly things, how can you possibly believe if I tell you about heavenly things? No one has ever gone to heaven and returned. But the Son of Man has come down from heaven. And as Moses lifted up the bronze snake on a pole in the wilderness, so the Son of Man must be lifted up, so that everyone who believes in him will have eternal life.

"For this is how God loved the world: He gave his one and only Son, so that everyone who believes in him will not perish but have eternal life. God sent his Son into the world not to judge the world, but to save the world through him.

"There is no judgment against anyone who believes in him. But anyone who does not believe in him has already been judged for not believing in God's one and only Son. And the judgment is based on this fact: God's light came into the world, but people loved the darkness more than the light, for their actions were evil. All who do evil hate the light and refuse to go near it for fear their sins will be exposed. But those who do what is right come to the light so others can see that they are doing what God wants.

John 14: 1-31

"Do not let your hearts be troubled. You believe in God; believe also in me [Jesus]. My Father's house has many rooms; if that were not so, would I have told you that I am going there to prepare a place for you? And if I go and prepare a place for you, I will come back and take you to be with me that you also may be where I am. You know the way to the place where I am going."

Thomas said to him, "Lord, we don't know where you are going, so how can we know the way?"

Jesus answered, "I am the way and the truth and the life. No one comes to the Father except through me. If you really know me, you will know my Father as well. From now on, you do know him and have seen him."

Philip said, "Lord, show us the Father and that will be enough for us."

Jesus answered: "Don't you know me, Philip, even after I have been among you such a long time? Anyone who has seen me has seen the Father. How can you say, 'Show us the Father'? Don't you believe that I am in the Father, and that the Father is in me? The words I say to you I do not speak on my own authority. Rather, it is the Father, living in me, who is doing his work. Believe me when I say that I am in the Father and the Father is in me; or at least believe on the evidence of the works themselves. Very truly I tell you, whoever believes in me will do the works I have been doing, and they will do even greater things than these, because I am going to the Father. And I will do whatever you ask in my name, so that the Father may be glorified in the Son. You may ask me for anything in my name, and I will do it.

"If you love me, keep my commands. And I will ask the Father, and he will give you another advocate to help you and be with you forever— the Spirit of truth. The world cannot accept him, because it neither sees him nor knows him. But you know him, for he lives with you and will be in you. I will not leave you as orphans; I will come to you. Before long, the world will not see me anymore, but you will see me. Because I live, you also will live. On that day you will realize that I am in my Father, and you are in me, and I am in you. Whoever has my commands and keeps them is the one who loves me. The one who loves me will be loved by my Father, and I too will love them and show myself to them."

Then Judas (not Judas Iscariot) said, "But, Lord, why do you intend to show yourself to us and not to the world?"

Jesus replied, "Anyone who loves me will obey my teaching. My Father will love them, and we will come to them and make our home with them. Anyone who does not love me will not obey my teaching. These words you hear are not my own; they belong to the Father who sent me.

"All this I have spoken while still with you. But the Advocate, the Holy Spirit, whom the Father will send in my name, will teach you all things and will remind you of everything I have said to you. Peace I leave with you; my peace I give you. I do not give to you as the world gives. Do not let your hearts be troubled and do not be afraid.

"You heard me say, 'I am going away and I am coming back to

you.' If you loved me, you would be glad that I am going to the Father, for the Father is greater than I. I have told you now before it happens, so that when it does happen you will believe. I will not say much more to you, for the prince of this world is coming. He has no hold over me, but he comes so that the world may learn that I love the Father and do exactly what my Father has commanded me.

Romans 1: 18-20
But God shows his anger from heaven against all sinful, wicked people who suppress the truth by their wickedness. They know the truth about God because he has made it obvious to them. For ever since the world was created, people have seen the earth and sky. Through everything God made, they can clearly see his invisible qualities—his eternal power and divine nature. So they have no excuse for not knowing God.

Romans 3:21-26
But now God has shown us a way to be made right with him without keeping the requirements of the law, as was promised in the writings of Moses and the prophets long ago. We are made right with God by placing our faith in Jesus Christ. And this is true for everyone who believes, no matter who we are.

For everyone has sinned; we all fall short of God's glorious standard. Yet God, in his grace, freely makes us right in his sight. He did this through Christ Jesus when he freed us from the penalty for our sins. For God presented Jesus as the sacrifice for sin. People are made right with God when they believe that Jesus sacrificed his life, shedding his blood. This sacrifice shows that God was being fair when he held back and did not punish those who sinned in times past, for he was looking ahead and including them in what he would do in this present time. God did this to demonstrate his righteousness, for he himself is fair and just, and he makes sinners right in his sight when they believe in Jesus.

Romans 10:5-15

For Moses writes that the law's way of making a person right with God requires obedience to all of its commands. But faith's way of getting right with God says, "Don't say in your heart, 'Who will go up to heaven?' (to bring Christ down to earth). And don't say, 'Who will go down to the place of the dead?' (to bring Christ back to life again)." In fact, it says,

"The message is very close at hand; it is on your lips and in your heart."

And that message is the very message about faith that we preach: If you openly declare that Jesus is Lord and believe in your heart that God raised him from the dead, you will be saved. For it is by believing in your heart that you are made right with God, and it is by openly declaring your faith that you are saved. As the Scriptures tell us, "Anyone who trusts in him will never be disgraced." Jew and Gentile are the same in this respect. They have the same Lord, who gives generously to all who call on him. For "Everyone who calls on the name of the Lord will be saved."

But how can they call on him to save them unless they believe in him? And how can they believe in him if they have never heard about him? And how can they hear about him unless someone tells them? And how will anyone go and tell them without being sent? That is why the Scriptures say, "How beautiful are the feet of messengers who bring good news!"

1 Thessalonians 5:9, 10

For God chose to save us through our Lord Jesus Christ, not to pour out his anger on us. Christ died for us so that, whether we are dead or alive when he returns, we can live with him forever.

Ephesians 2:1-10

Once you were dead because of your disobedience and your many sins. You used to live in sin, just like the rest of the world, obeying the devil—the commander of the powers in the unseen world. He is the spirit at work in the hearts of those who refuse to obey God. All of us used to live that way, following the passionate desires and inclinations of our sinful nature. By our very nature we were subject to God's anger, just like everyone else.

But God is so rich in mercy, and he loved us so much, that even though we were dead because of our sins, he gave us life when he raised Christ from the dead. (It is only by God's grace that you have been saved!) For he raised us from the dead along with Christ and seated us with him in the heavenly realms because we are united with Christ Jesus. So God can point to us in all future ages as examples of the incredible wealth of his grace and kindness toward us, as shown in all he has done for us who are united with Christ Jesus.

God saved you by his grace when you believed. And you can't take credit for this; it is a gift from God. Salvation is not a reward for the good things we have done, so none of us can boast about it. For we are God's masterpiece. He has created us anew in Christ Jesus, so we can do the good things he planned for us long ago.

Hebrews 1-2

Long ago God spoke many times and in many ways to our ancestors through the prophets. And now in these final days, he has spoken to us through his Son. God promised everything to the Son as an inheritance, and through the Son he created the universe. The Son radiates God's own glory and expresses the very character of God, and he sustains everything by the mighty power of his command. When he had cleansed us from our sins, he sat down in the place of honor at the right hand of the majestic God in heaven. This shows that the Son is far greater than the angels, just as the name God gave him is greater than their names.

For God never said to any angel what he said to Jesus:
"You are my Son.
Today I have become your Father."
God also said,
"I will be his Father,
and he will be my Son."
And when he brought his supreme Son into the world, God said,

"Let all of God's angels worship him."
Regarding the angels, he says,
"He sends his angels like the winds,
his servants like flames of fire."
But to the Son he says,
"Your throne, O God, endures forever and ever.
You rule with a scepter of justice.
You love justice and hate evil.
Therefore, O God, your God has anointed you,
pouring out the oil of joy on you more than on anyone else."
He also says to the Son,
"In the beginning, Lord, you laid the foundation of the earth
and made the heavens with your hands. They will perish, but you remain forever.
They will wear out like old clothing. You will fold them up like a cloak
and discard them like old clothing.
But you are always the same;
you will live forever."
And God never said to any of the angels,
"Sit in the place of honor at my right hand
until I humble your enemies,
making them a footstool under your feet."
Therefore, angels are only servants—spirits sent to care for people who will inherit salvation.

So we must listen very carefully to the truth we have heard, or we may drift away from it. For the message God delivered through angels has always stood firm, and every violation of the law and every act of disobedience was punished. So what makes us think we can escape if we ignore this great salvation that was first announced by the Lord Jesus himself and then delivered to us by those who heard him speak? And God confirmed the message by giving signs and wonders and various miracles and gifts of the Holy Spirit whenever he chose.

And furthermore, it is not angels who will control the future world

we are talking about. For in one place the Scriptures say,
"What are mere mortals that you should think about them,
or a son of man that you should care for him?
Yet for a little while you made them a little lower than the angels
and crowned them with glory and honor.

You gave them authority over all things."

Now when it says "all things," it means nothing is left out. But we have not yet seen all things put under their authority. What we do see is Jesus, who for a little while was given a position "a little lower than the angels"; and because he suffered death for us, he is now "crowned with glory and honor." Yes, by God's grace, Jesus tasted death for everyone. God, for whom and through whom everything was made, chose to bring many children into glory. And it was only right that he should make Jesus, through his suffering, a perfect leader, fit to bring them into their salvation.

So now Jesus and the ones he makes holy have the same Father. That is why Jesus is not ashamed to call them his brothers and sisters. For he said to God,

"I will proclaim your name to my brothers and sisters.
I will praise you among your assembled people."

He also said, "I will put my trust in him," that is, "I and the children God has given me."

Because God's children are human beings—made of flesh and blood—the Son also became flesh and blood. For only as a human being could he die, and only by dying could he break the power of the devil, who had the power of death. Only in this way could he set free all who have lived their lives as slaves to the fear of dying.

We also know that the Son did not come to help angels; he came to help the descendants of Abraham. Therefore, it was necessary for him to be made in every respect like us, his brothers and sisters, so that he could be our merciful and faithful High Priest before God. Then he could offer a sacrifice that would take away the sins of the people. Since he himself has gone through suffering and testing, he is able to help us when we are being tested.

Made in the USA
Lexington, KY
09 November 2017